PRESENTS

50
LIFE LESSONS
FROM
INSPIRING
WOMEN

LYNN W. MURPHY, M.ED.

Keeping pushing the limits.

Lynn Murphy

Flint Hills Publishing

March 202X

⫙Flint Hills Publishing

Topeka, Kansas
www.flinthillspublishing.com

Ebook ISBN 978-1-953583-19-2
Paperback ISBN 978-1-953583-20-8

Library of Congress Control Number: 2021923015

Printed in the U.S.A.

CONTENTS

This book is dedicated to the 50 inspiring women who shared their stories, and to ambitious women everywhere who strive to find their voice, speak their truth, and change the world.

.

Introduction

Lynn W. Murphy
Founder of Women Who Push the Limits

During a virtual mini reunion with high school classmates a few months ago, I announced I was writing this book. After a long pause, one curious classmate I hadn't seen for decades tentatively inquired, "Have you ever written a book before?" What was left unsaid was, "We all know how old you are. What made you decide to start writing books NOW?" I laughed. Good question. But why not now?

My coach of many years, Connie H. Deutsch, has been pushing me for decades to write a book. She had more confidence in my ability to write a book than I did. I started writing one years ago, but I soon lost interest. Then a couple of years ago she started pushing me again to put myself out there with a book, and to show up bigger in the world. I have taught customer service, team building, and communication for nearly two decades, but the thought of writing about those topics ranked high on the yawn factor. Lots of people have written those books. I couldn't get excited about writing another. Connie suggested I write about something that really interests me and that would be important for others to read—empowering women. Record numbers of women were running for political office. Women's voices were being heard more all the time. It felt like the right time and the right topic.

Since then, I've conducted in-depth Zoom interviews with these 50 remarkable women you're about to meet. In rich and insightful conversations, they shared their fascinating stories, their life lessons, and their wise advice about pushing the limits.

With COVID impacting the world, it turned out to be a perfect time to interview and write. Many of us were staying home and had learned to use Zoom, so we had the time and the technology to make it happen.

I had originally intended to take all 50 stories and their lessons from the seventy-plus hours of interview transcripts and weave them together into one book.

But as I worked with the transcripts, I realized I could not do justice to the wealth of important experiences and variety of topics from all 50 interviews in just one book. There is enough material for several books. Everyone's story is compelling, and I could not choose which to include and which to exclude from the original project concept.

It became clear that the book you're reading now needed to come first as a way to include all 50 women and introduce you to each of them, leaving nobody out.

To use the term made popular during the pandemic, *I pivoted*. With the blessing and encouragement of my exceptionally wise and infinitely patient publisher, Thea Rademacher, I've taken short sections from all 50 interviews for this book.

Here you'll find a chapter about each of the 50 women, with an abbreviated portion of her story, a significant lesson from her life, and her advice for pushing your own limits even farther.

In this book, you'll get a taste for what is to come in the longer interview books. Once your appetite has been whetted, I know you'll be eager for the next course. The themed book, or books, is next on my list to write.

Each rich, fascinating conversation was so different from the next. And each one was a treasure trove of wisdom. I was often pleasantly surprised by the women's willingness to be so authentic and vulnerable.

You'll find a wide variety of limit-pushing situations in the stories here. Some involve overcoming physical challenges—either voluntarily or out of necessity. Others involve intellectual, emotional, or situational limits. The courage, resilience, and faith with which each woman has shown up is inspirational.

In these stories, the women reflect about finding their voice, speaking their truth, and changing the world.

Some of the women in this book will be familiar to you. Others' lives may not have intersected with yours yet. Each has powerful stories. You will identify with these stories—maybe not in the exact way the situations played out in the women's lives—but in ways that you can relate to your own life. These stories will inspire you to push your own limits. It's a privilege to serve as a conduit for bringing the voices of these women to a wider audience.

I knew some of the women before interviewing them, and the interviews deepened our relationships. With the women I had never met, our conversation quickly created genuine bonds. I would never have connected with many of these women if I hadn't had the excuse of writing this book. Warm friendships that continue to enrich my life have developed with a few of these former strangers and will continue long after I'm through writing these books.

I was thrilled—and pleasantly surprised—when these extremely busy women agreed to do the interview, especially the ones who didn't know me. That speaks to the appeal of this topic more than to my power of persuasion.

Frequently, as we were winding up an interview, a woman would say something like, "I don't usually share that part of my story." It was an honor that they trusted me enough to be open and candid about their lives and their challenges, and that they are willing to share their story with you. Their authenticity and vulnerability will touch your heart as they have touched mine. I trust that you'll feel the connections too.

I encourage you to follow their example and let your authenticity and vulnerability show. When we acknowledge our humanness and imperfections, we can love ourselves and each other more genuinely.

Writing this book has pushed me way outside my comfort zone and has taken me on an amazing adventure, one I never imagined at the beginning. I'm filled with excitement and doubt. I love getting to know other women. I feel creative and satisfied when I write a paragraph that pleases me. I wonder if I'm doing it right. Ah, yes, there's that perfection gene wagging its finger in my face. One of these days, I'll leave that critter gasping for its last breath as I abandon my misconception that I must not only do it right, but I must do it perfectly the first time.

And because these stories have been carved out of long interviews, I have not always used the women's exact words. I have done my best to stay true to each woman's message while presenting her thoughts in a readable way. Any mistakes of fact are mine, not the interviewee's, and certainly are not intended to misrepresent the intention of what the woman shared.

My life has been enriched beyond measure by the heartfelt connections with these women, their stories, their authenticity, their vulnerability, and their trust—most of all their trust.

I am so very grateful to all of them for being part of this project, and to you for reading this book.

Let these stories inspire you and motivate you to push your own limits even farther than you have already as you **find your voice, speak your truth, and change the world**.

Your Challenges Are Gifts

Debbie Allen

Find the gifts in the difficult things you go through. Those challenges, those roadblocks, those obstacles that we all have in front of us, are really gifts. When you look at them as lessons and learn from them, you will become stronger and more confident.

It was a gift to me that my first husband decided to get somebody else pregnant while I was on fertility drugs. I can't imagine still being married to that cheater and stuck back in Indiana where I felt so disconnected. It was a gift that my second husband taught me so much about growing a business before he turned abusive and threatened to kill me. Terrified, I walked away from everything in order to be safe. I escaped with great gifts from those hard lessons—how to make it on my own. And I found my amazing, **amazing,** third and forever husband.

When a woman holds on to her victimhood and keeps repeating those oh-poor-me stories, I just want to get away from her. That is certainly not a woman who's ever going to ever push her limits. Stop hanging on to the stories that don't serve you. Stop being in victim mode. Find your strength and your power.

These experiences and others really toughened me up. I might not look like I'm a tough chick—a little 5'2" blond-haired girl—but I'm confident I can hold my own in almost any situation. You really know who you are when you've come to appreciate how you've dealt with those really scary things that happened in your life.

Every time I get fearful, I look back at the gutsy things I did where I pushed the limits. When you're fearful, go back to those moments when you were brave, and say, "Hey, if I could do that, I can do this!"

When you want to quit, remember that whatever you're going through is a temporary thing. Don't sabotage your success by making a bad decision because you're acting out of emotion. When you're emotional, that is not a time to make quick judgments.

Women need to learn to take that emotion away and look at realities. I'm a very common-sense, down-to-earth, reality person. When something looks scary or weird, I use common sense to break it down to the reality of the situation. Then I deal with that reality.

A lot of women look at me and think I'm so confident. Well, I can be confident because of all that I've gone through. It's not that I can just take this magic confidence pill. I've taken risks and pushed the limits from a very young age and have the gift of confidence, among other things, to show for it.

What we all want is confidence. That's where it starts for us. When a woman has confidence—look out. She's powerful!

Learn what you can from every situation even if you've got to walk away from it.

I've had times where I couldn't stay in a situation because things that were happening went against my core values. I've walked away from friendships, marriages, and business partnerships when they weren't working. I call that *bless and release*.

I left a long-time friendship when she became negative and self-destructive. It was hard, but I just couldn't be with her anymore. I had to be true to myself.

I left two marriages where I didn't feel valued and wasn't

treated with respect. I said what was true for me, and I left.

I've ended partnerships when it became clear that our work ethics were very different or when we didn't share the same core values. My values are too important to me.

I had all my eggs in one basket when I left a partnership and had no income for a while. But it was more important to me to walk away and start again when I saw that it wasn't the right fit. The gift was the push I needed to assess my skills and reinvent everything.

It is hard to walk away from people you're bonded to in business and friendship. But it's vital to speak up when things aren't in alignment with your values. When it's hard to speak your mind, that's when you need to do it more.

When I saw someone in business misrepresenting things, I called them out. I stood up and spoke up to a group of high-powered, multi-millionaire men who are well-known in the industry. I called them out on what they were doing and ended my association with them.

Don't hold back and be a wallflower or use an excuse like, *Maybe it'll all work out*, or *Maybe I don't have to be the one to speak up this time*.

Speaking up builds your confidence. When you build your confidence, you're powerful and your confidence will draw more opportunities and more success to you.

When you're faced with an obstacle, find a way to keep pushing the limits. That will build your confidence when you get through it. You can be scared—scared as hell—when you're pushing through it. But when you get on the other side, you're like, *Okay, I've got this!*

Look at your stories and ask yourself, *What lessons did I learn? What were the gifts?* I know I'm a different person today because I'm on the other side of so many challenges. I'm stronger. Strength and confidence are some of the gifts that your challenges hand you.

❄ ❄ ❄

Debbie Allen, also known as The Expert of Experts, is an internationally-recognized business growth and market positioning expert. She has been a professional speaker and business mentor for 25 years and presented before thousands of people in 28 countries. She earned the coveted designation of Certified Speaking Professional from the National Speakers Association. Debbie is a bestselling author of nine books, including *The Highly Paid Expert,* and hosts the *Access to Experts Podcast*. She is a VIP contributor for *Entrepreneur Magazine*, and an award-winning entrepreneur who has built and sold numerous million-dollar companies in diverse industries.

www.DebbieAllen.com

If It's Right for You, Persist

Hepsharat Amadi, M.D.

In my freshman year at Harvard, we had to declare what we were planning to major in. Like me, a lot of students declared a pre-med major. But by the end of the undergraduate experience, so many turned away from that. Some had gotten involved in other things they liked more. But many gave up on medical school because they were discouraged by other people saying, "Medical school is going to be so competitive. It's going to be something that you really can't handle." They bought into someone else's opinion, and they gave up on their dream.

Many times, I have challenged other people's opinions. I'm a very stubborn, persistent person. If somebody tells me I can't do something, that gives me more incentive to prove that I can.

When I applied to Bronx High School of Science, a highly-ranked specialized school, people told me, "Oh, that's such a hard entrance exam to pass. You probably won't pass it." I sat for the exam anyway—and I passed.

For college, I wanted to go to Harvard. Again people—even my guidance counselor—told me, "Oh, don't bother applying there because you had an only an 89 average in science, and they don't accept anybody at Harvard who has less than a 90." I was not going to give up on my dream, especially for just a one-point score.

Fortunately, I was blessed with parents who really believed in me and encouraged me to go after my dream. And yes, I was pretty happy when I got in.

In my freshman year at Harvard, I had difficulty adjusting to the pace of those crazy pre-med classes, having to study in ways that were different than how I studied in high school. I didn't do well my first year, and as a result, had to take a year off.

When it was time to apply for medical school, I showed my portfolio to a man who was on the board of directors of a medical school. Even though my grades improved my later years at Harvard, he told me I wasn't ready to apply to medical school. He recommended I take another year of courses first.

I thought to myself, *No! I'm going to apply now. I'm not getting any younger. The worst they can say to me is no.* After going through that complex process and submitting applications to many different medical schools, I got **one** acceptance back. Along with the acceptance came a requirement that I pass a year of calculus with at least a C.

I never intended to take another math class ever again. But I took a year of calculus—differential and then integral—and passed both with a C. Those were the hardest Cs I've ever gotten. In retrospect, I'm glad that I put myself through it. It gave me a more accurate idea of my own mental resources. It made me realize that if I was desperate enough, I could even do the math.

I was excited to attend what turned out to be a progressive medical school where women made up 30% of the incoming class. In 1983, that was a lot.

Long before I got into medical school, I learned to be a critical thinker. Both my parents were journalists. They taught me how to analyze information, how to read between the lines, and how to consider on whose behalf this information was being presented.

From the beginning, I questioned ideas. My approach to medicine was not that of conventional doctors.

I went into medicine with the goal of not just helping people manage the illness they had, but rather to prevent them from having any serious illnesses, and to help raise their level of health. I never was under the delusion that I could take a healthy person and make them healthier by giving them medication or doing surgery on them. I wanted to take a person who was already healthy and help them to be healthier. That's not something you can do with conventional medicine.

At one time I thought I might become a psychiatrist. In medical school, I discovered that if you have physical things going on, you're going to have mental and emotional things going on. And if you have mental and emotional things going on, you're going to have physical things going on. You can't separate them any more than you can separate the head side of the coin from the tail side. It all goes together. I knew becoming a doctor would allow me to do what I wanted to do—treat the whole person.

I always approached medicine from this wholistic perspective. It was a matter of gathering the tools that would best enable me to practice in a way that I would like.

A few years out from residency, I went back to school for acupuncture and Chinese herbs. Later, being introduced to a quantum biofeedback machine completely changed my life, my family's life, my patients' lives, and my view of reality. I used to look at things from a much more Newtonian perspective. Now I look at things more from an energetic quantum perspective.

Quantum biofeedback allows me to interact with all aspects of the patient—the physical, mental, emotional, and spiritual. It makes me happy that I can truly treat each person as a unique individual, and not just as a diseased entity.

I was fortunate enough to have parents who taught me to think for myself. They believed in me and encouraged me to do what I knew was right for me.

Don't let anyone tell you can't do something. Follow your intuition. That's my compass. I've learned that when I don't follow my intuition, I mess up. When I follow my intuition, it works out.

If you believe it's right for you, **persist**. Believe in yourself and claim your dream.

❀ ❀ ❀

Hepsharat Amadi, M.D. is a medical doctor in private practice in Coral Springs, Florida. She is trained in both Chinese and Western medicine and offers alternative medicine in her *wholistic* family practice. She treats the whole body and works with her patients as a team to optimize their physical, mental, emotional, and spiritual wellbeing. She keeps her patients healthy by using quantum biofeedback, bioidentical hormone replacement, nutritional supplements, and lifestyle counseling, and by referring patients to appropriate allied health practitioners. Dr. Amadi uses Western medicine where it is appropriate and necessary to stabilize her patient, thus giving more time for natural methods to work.

www.greatnaturaldoctor.com

Passion Makes Your Dream Come True

Christine Blosdale

When you feel passionate about something, you already have a fuel, a fire, a propulsion behind you to make it real. There is nothing in this world that can compare to your energy and your unique signature. Whatever it is that you want to do, whether it's with business, family, or relationships, you have your own unique voice and you have your own unique spin.

Right now is the perfect time to step out and to do something that you're passionate about.

Forever I've had a desire to write a book. Even though growing up my mother and grandmother always told me I could do anything, I didn't know if I could do this. The thought of writing hundreds of pages seemed like a really daunting process. I thought I had to use a typewriter and wear a smoking jacket and fedora like Sam Spade. It scared me. I wasn't sure I would ever make it happen.

Because I was so passionate about this goal, I kept seeing my photo on the back cover of a book. But I didn't know how I was going to get there. So, I practiced what I teach my clients—I pretended it had already happened. I deeply felt my passion and my excitement about being a successful author. I put my vision out into the Universe.

Then, at Craig Duswalt's Rockstar Marketing Bootcamp, I met Suzy Prudden, an amazing publisher. It was sort of the perfect storm. She gave me a simple formula to follow that did not include smoking jackets, fedoras, old typewriters, or hundreds of pages. It was not a daunting process. I only had to write 35 pages on a subject that I'm passionate about—how to get started in podcasting. It's my own words. When you read it, you can feel it's me—it's my voice.

And now in my 50s, I became an international number one Amazon bestselling author of *Your Amazing Itty Bitty® Podcast Book—The Top 15 Reasons Why You Need to Tap into the Power and Profits of Podcasting*. It wasn't the daunting process I feared. It was easy. It's a subject that I'm passionate about because I want to help others get started in podcasting. It was a joy to write it.

I have also manifested my dream relationship. I'm now living in New South Wales, Australia, with my wife and our children. If you had told me a few years ago this was going to be my life, I would have said you were crazy.

I had never been married before. I never wanted to live out my old age with someone before. I was perfectly happy living in LA. But as soon as I met Tracy, I knew she was my human—who lived 7,000 miles away. We had obstacle after obstacle after obstacle. All we knew was that we loved each other and wanted to be together. We had to overcome the distance. We had to overcome the time zones. We had to overcome the fact that in Australia, same-sex marriage was not legal. It has become legal since we've been together, but it wasn't when we first met. We married in the United States, but because of our job commitments and Tracy's children, we continued to live on separate continents.

Then COVID hit.

When things started to shut down, Tracy urged me to get a flight as soon as possible. My goosebumps were telling me this was what I was supposed to do. I was on the phone with the airlines for an hour. I must have had panic in my voice as I told the representative, "I **have** to get there to be with my wife and our children during this pandemic." I got a beautifully sympathetic representative who worked with me and worked with me. Finally, she said, "There's one flight left—in a couple hours. Do you want it?" I said, "What do you think?!"

I ended up on the last flight allowed into Australia from Los Angeles before the lockdown. I had two hours to throw everything in a suitcase, lock up my house, and get to the airport. I called my boss. I called my mom. I went to the bank. I don't know how I did it, but I did it.

We wanted to live together, but we didn't know how to do it. It took a worldwide pandemic to push us to make it happen in a few hours. I am grateful and happy that I'm here with her and our children. I'm exactly where I'm supposed to be, and where I want to be. Everything I left behind is just stuff.

Never give up what you're really passionate about. You may encounter obstacles here and there. You may have to bob and weave. You may have to do the Matrix move. When you come from a place of high intention and from your heart, the Universe makes a way. Things open up. Maybe you'll end up sitting next to somebody at a restaurant who has the key to the next step you need to take. I needed to meet my publisher at a marketing event in order to get my book written. I accidentally came upon Tracy's Instagram and now we're married.

Your vision—whether it's a book, a podcast, a business, or a relationship—already exists in a parallel universe. It's there waiting for you to claim it.

The most important lesson I've learned in my life is the power of our thoughts and our visions. It's extremely important to understand that we literally create the reality that we are living in. It's easy to get caught up in things, to get knocked off guard, and to become wrapped up in fear. What you focus on every single day has incredible power.

Infuse your dream with passion and focus on it. It's never too late to make it come true.

❋ ❋ ❋

Christine Blosdale is a podcast and multimedia coach, international three-time Amazon #1 bestselling author, media personality, and engaging speaker. She has 25 years of experience in the entertainment world as a broadcast journalist, interviewer, and award-winning radio personality. She has raised over $19 million for KPFK, the nonprofit radio station in Los Angeles. She hosts and produces two podcasts: *Out of the Box with Christine: The Podcast for Conscious Entrepreneurs*, and *The Micro Podcast on Podcasting*. Her workshops, podcast academy, and coaching programs are helping her clients around the world promote their products and services while making their dreams come true.

www.ChristineBlosdale.com

Gratitude, Gratitude, Gratitude

Bridget Brady

We all have those days where everywhere we turn is crap. Those times when we're feeling that engine of anger and upset and hate starting to rev. These aren't deep feelings of fear; we're just whining and complaining. Go ahead. Have a short pity party—just don't invite anyone else to your party! Then, step back, and get into gratitude. Take a breath. Remember what you're grateful for. Do a *gratitude storm* with yourself and think of all the things you're grateful for, then return to a state of gratitude.

Here's how a gratitude practice saved my life. . .

In 2010, I was so sick of working in a cubicle, working for someone else as a consultant. There was this feeling inside of me that this wasn't really what I wanted to be doing. I told myself, I told the Universe, I told God, that owning my own business was my dream.

The economy was changing and the major lending institution I consulted for—in fact, the entire industry—was going through severe cutbacks and changes. Friday morning I came into work, logged in, and opened an email that said:

Dear Miss Brady,
Thank you so much for your eight years of excellent service. Today is your last day.

Just like that. No notice. No severance. No nothing. Pack up your stuff. Thank you so much. Don't bill us anymore. You're done.

I had no job, I had no savings. My boyfriend left and took all our furniture. I lost everything. I moved from my beautiful beach condo to the smallest, crappiest apartment in the Inland Empire.

For two months, I laid on my floor with my laptop—the only place I could with no furniture—watching free Hulu. I fell into deep depression. My life was over.

One day, I woke up and said to myself, *You know, Bridget, you have been telling yourself, telling the Universe, telling God, that you want to start your own business. Maybe this was the Universe's answer.* That wasn't exactly how I expected the answer to be delivered.

Then a dear friend suggested I start writing *gratitude pages.* At the beginning, it felt almost impossible to fill even one page of things I was grateful for. I was dead broke—again. *How did I get here—again? What do I have to be grateful for?* I was barely eating. I was laying on a bare floor with no job, no relationship, not even furniture. I literally started writing things like: *I'm grateful for my sight. I'm grateful that I can walk.* That led me to some things that seemed silly: *I'm grateful for my beautiful skin.* I went deeper to: *I'm super grateful for my family.* And suddenly, after writing something down day after day that I was grateful for, magic started to happen.

I told myself to take one tiny action forward at a time. I started with the tiniest—and I mean the tiniest—steps: getting up and taking a shower, making myself some soup. Once I took one tiny step, I realized I could do three other things. More gratitude. Then I could do this one other little thing. *It's not that big of a deal.* Before I knew it, I was doing 10 other things. I slowly, but surely, started to spiral up, writing more and more in my gratitude pages each day.

I had been stuck looking at the whole humongous goal:

starting my own business, winning a Grammy, becoming a millionaire. *All of that is so daunting. How do I do that?* It came down to tiny little actions forward, one at a time, and feeling deep gratitude for each and every step no matter how small.

Being an entrepreneur in my new business gave me more freedom. I started singing again and produced my album, *Choose to Forgive,* which was considered for a Grammy.

My first entrepreneur teacher, T. Harv Ecker, says, "What you focus on expands." Once I focused on what I was grateful for, my world expanded. The Universe listens. It gives us gifts in packages we don't always recognize.

Express your vision to the Universe and express your gratitude for the gifts you receive. Then watch your world expand.

Bridget Brady is an enlightened entrepreneur, speaker, #1 international bestselling author, and social media and online marketing authority. She spent years in theater in New York City and worked in film and television in Los Angeles. She's been in the information technology industry for over 25 years, spending seven of those years in New York City working on Wall Street. She founded a full-service, custom, online marketing agency, **Amp Up My Biz,** as a way to escape the corporate America "prison" and rat race she felt trapped in. She helps entrepreneurs and business owners get the tools they need to catapult their business success.

www.ampupmybiz.com

Give Yourself Permission to Make Mistakes

Susan L. Brooks

Mistakes are your best way to learn because you're not going to make the same ones again. If you go back and make the same mistakes over and over, then there's a problem.

When we owned Cookies From Home, one of our staff rolled the cinnamon sugar cookies in salt. I don't know how long it took us to realize that every cinnamon cookie that went out was with cinnamon salt instead of cinnamon sugar.

When an employee made a mistake, my process was to sit and talk with the employee and debrief the situation. We would talk about the lessons learned. Then in a staff meeting, I would have that person stand up and tell the story of their mistake, so it didn't always come from me. It would come from the team. I think it meant more that way. Then I would ask the question, "What did you learn?" That way the entire staff could benefit from that one mistake.

Because we were serving food, we had considerable risk. We were at attention all the time. If there was a way to do it differently, or if there was a way to do it better, that was our goal. The main thing was it had to ooze excellence. That was nonnegotiable. That helped us grow.

Don't let the fear of making a mistake stop you from moving forward. Take a risk. Create a clear vision and go for it. It's important to ask yourself how you would feel if you didn't do it. Give yourself permission to step into that vision.

Once, over Christmas and New Year's, I was on a tour in Israel with my family. We ended up at Masada, an ancient fortress on a mountaintop that was thought to be unassailable. We had the opportunity to climb this mountain. It's 1,500 feet straight up. Everybody on the tour was much younger than us. And those that were our age were infirm and couldn't climb it. But my husband and I who are in our 70s, stood at the base of that mountain, and I said, "I'm going to climb this."

My son was saying, "Don't hurt yourself, Mom. Your knees aren't that great. I don't know if you should do this." And I thought about being on the bus going back to our hotel, and wondered, how would I feel if I didn't do this? I couldn't imagine not doing it. I was going to give it my best and not worry about what might happen.

And I did—1,500 feet straight up. I was not the first to get to the top. I wasn't even the fifth. I was the last. But I made it.

When I struggle today, when I think about the challenges of the day, I think about that mountain. In my life I've climbed many, many mountains, and I got there. So that mountain of Masada is helping me get through today and tomorrow. I pushed the limits, and I did it.

I live my life like Wonder Woman. I ask myself, *What would you do today if you were brave?* Be brave. Take those risks. Climb those mountains. Make those mistakes and grow stronger because of them.

❊ ❊ ❊

Susan L. Brooks is a business growth strategist, international speaker, author, mentor, and change agent. As an innovative, award-winning entrepreneur, Susan built a 30-year, multimillion-dollar business (and sold it!). She draws on her business expertise and real-deal experiences when working with her business clients and audiences. Women business owners especially hire Susan to get their business on the fast track to a profitable and sustainable company. Always a trailblazer and an activist for women, Susan founded the Phoenix chapter of the National Association of Women Business Owners (NAWBO) in 1975. Never one to stop pushing her limits, Susan's newest topic under development is about changing the face of aging. Stay tuned for news about the extraordinary programs she is creating.

www.susanlbrooks.com

Go For It!

Minda Burr

Every person in the world has desires, dreams, and curiosities that they may or may not admit to themselves. Yet they might not go for it because they're afraid of failing. Or they're afraid they're not good enough. Or they hear that little voice in their head: *Who am I to think that I can do this?* Do you relate to this?

Are you one of those people who lives their life wanting to please other people, whether it's to please your parents, or impress your friends, or to do only what you know is expected of you?

That's prison.

I have not lived my life the way everyone else has. When I graduated from college in the 70s, most of my friends were getting married and having kids. I knew early on that was not my path. In fact, I didn't get married until I was 69, when I found the man I wanted to spend the rest of my life with.

In my teens, I was a competitive athlete and loved winning. My passion to compete turned into a thirst for adventure. I've always been curious about everything, and I've very much been led by my instincts rather than the status quo. That's been my saving grace. When I have an impulse to do something, I follow it. I don't go into fear about it. It boils down to: Will I love doing it, and will it be fun?

I chose jobs that would be exciting for a young, feisty gal. I dealt blackjack in Lake Tahoe so I could make money to backpack around Europe for four months. I managed a club in Hawaii—the hottest club in Waikiki. But I could only party hearty for so long. I decided to get my master's degree in drama. I made a quick decision, packed my bags, and flew back to Tucson. I was 30 years old when I started acting.

When acting wasn't enough of a creative outlet, I founded a theater company, produced and directed several plays, and then wrote, produced, and directed my own play. I even raised the money for the play in just two weeks. When I'm passionate about something, I hyperfocus and shift into high gear.

I briefly worked as a hypnotherapist, but soon got bored with that. So, I created an acting class for professional people who wanted to take an acting class, but they were too nervous to do it with professional actors. Within a week, I put together an improv class made up of incredible, successful people: doctors, lawyers, a minister, a doctor of oriental medicine, real estate agents, and advertising executives. They wanted to have fun, and for five years we had a blast.

When I was in my 50s, I started my jewelry company, determined to do it my way—the fun way. I never took a jewelry class, I just started experimenting. Instead of walking into stores and begging them to carry my jewelry, I created social gatherings—high-end cocktail parties—and invited fabulous out-there women who love fashion and love getting compliments. While a hundred people are drinking wine, laughing, trying on the jewelry, and telling each other which pieces look absolutely fabulous on them, I just socialize and sip my martini. I don't have to sell a thing. The women sell it to each other. And we all have fun.

My mother was my inspiration and my role model. She was a flight nurse in World War II, and my dad was a flight surgeon in the Pacific. For them, it was "live for today for tomorrow you may die." She was a real go-getter. Nobody was more outgoing or brave or courageous. Mom always told me, "If you're going to do something, go full out. Go for it." No matter what I wanted to do, she was so supportive. That's where I get my authentic enthusiasm for life.

I was born with a creative spirit and continue to do the things I love. And I do them my way—without giving in to doubts and fears.

Fear of failure is caring too much what other people might think, if for some reason, it doesn't work out. Give up caring about what anybody else thinks. Don't let those negative thoughts talk you out of something that you get excited about. Go for it. Express your unique creativity. If you've ever wanted to take an art class or a dance class, do it. You don't have to be the best artist in the world. Just be you. Everybody has their own signature way of creating art. Get out there and take a class or do something just for fun.

Do something wild and crazy. Plan a vacation to someplace exotic you've never been before. Some people go back to the same vacation spot every year. Really? When I'm going on a trip, I'm going to go someplace I haven't been before and experience something I've never experienced before.

I plan on being the Grandma Moses of jewelry, yet I know there are new interests and talents that I haven't discovered yet. That's the way it's always been. I'll pay attention to those next impulses.

Don't show up on your deathbed wishing you had had more fun in your life, or had enjoyed life more, or had done more of what you had a secret desire for. Stay open to discovering new talents and new gifts that you don't even know you have yet. The best is yet to come.

Go for it! Stop paying attention to what others think. There are naysayers out there—don't listen to them. If you want to try something, don't let anybody talk you out of it. Do it your way. Keep enjoying life. Keep creating. And, most of all, keep having fun.

❄ ❄ ❄

Minda Burr is a popular jewelry designer and owner of Minda Burr Jewelry. Her enthusiastic collectors are spread across the world, from Hollywood to London and Italy. She was featured in *Power Magazine,* which honors women doing exciting things in the world. Minda has been a competitive athlete, blackjack dealer, hypnotherapist, and avid world traveler. She expressed her creative spirit for many years as an actress, then co-founder, artistic director, playwright, and producer at the popular Alliance Repertory Company in Los Angeles. What's more inspiring, she didn't start making jewelry until she was in her early 50s. Along with her passion for jewelry, one of her current joys is spearheading popular memoir writing classes. Throughout her life, Minda has found adventure, creativity, and fun in everything she does.

Instagram: minda_burr_jewelry.

Speaking is the #1 Way to Build Your Business

Toni Caruso

The number one way to build your business is to speak on stage. It's a great way to show up as an expert in your field because anyone who is on the stage with a mic in their hand is perceived as an expert.

The opportunities for women right now are unlimited. But often women are afraid to step onto that stage. Instead of sharing their brilliance, they're hiding in their room, guarding all their knowledge, and resisting trying something new. Then they complain that their business is going nowhere.

Stop hiding.

There are people out there who need to hear the message you have to share. If you're nervous about sharing your passion from the stage, don't think about yourself—think about all the people your message will help.

You don't have to know everything before you take that leap. You just have to have a confidence inside that says, *I can do this.* If it keeps you up at night, and you're scared, then you're doing the right thing—then you're moving forward.

If I had only done the things that I felt I was comfortable doing, I'd be doing small, 25- to 50-person women's events in my neighborhood. Instead, I'm doing multi-day events with several hundred people all over the country.

Don't be afraid to take the plunge. Ask yourself, what's the worst thing that could happen? What's the best thing that can happen?

Here are some ways you can use speaking to grow your business:

You can host your own events. This works best if you have a large, loyal following. Always carefully consider the upfront costs involved. You will be responsible for all the details. You will contract to pay for the facility, and it's up to you to get people in the room who will spend money to help you pay for the event.

When I host my own event or produce an event for other people, a lot of little things keep me up at night. *What if I miss something?* If I do, I know I can figure out how to fix it. I do whatever I have to do to make this right. I don't get upset. I don't get mad. I say to myself, *All right, what do I have to do to make it work?* And then I get it done.

To overcome that stress, I take a few breaths, go outside and get some sunshine, and think it out. There's always a solution. If you don't know what to do, find someone who does and have them help you. There's nothing wrong with getting support.

Another way to get on stage is to "pay to play" and speak at someone else's event. Instead of paying upfront costs for your own event, you put your money toward paying to speak on another organizer's stage. If they are bringing 100 to 150 people that are your ideal clients, why not pay to be on that stage? During your speech, offer a program or service for a fee so the audience can work with you in the future. And best yet, you get to keep the money from whatever you sell.

There are also opportunities for you to get on stage for free, and then give a percentage of your sales to the organizer. Let's say you're selling a program that's $500. You agreed that the host gets 20% of every program you sell. So, the host is making money, $100 from each sale you make, and you're making $400 without having to make an upfront investment.

Other times you can speak for free but are not allowed to make an offer to sell something from the stage. In this case, your best bet is to have a freebie to give away. Tell the audience you would love to give each of them your ebook or a PDF if they will fill out a form. Your freebies should be electronic, so they cost you nothing but are irresistible to your target audience. You get to walk away with all those email addresses just for giving them something for free. Add them to your email nurturing campaign and follow up. You can offer your products or services over time as they get to know you.

And then there's the stage switch. If you host an event, you can invite qualified people to speak on your stage, and in return, they invite you to speak on their stage. Both of you keep the profits from whatever you sell.

Remember, you need to practice your speech. Don't go out for your first time and pay $5,000 to speak on a stage. You're going to make mistakes. Practice what you're going to say so that you're comfortable without reading it. There's nothing wrong with inviting your friends over and saying, *Hey, I'm going to give a speech. Can I practice on you?* If they're really your friends, they'll let you.

There are lots of ways that you can get visibility and build your speaking skills by speaking for free. There are Rotary Clubs, Chambers of Commerce, and Meetup groups. If you don't feel comfortable right away, improve your speaking skills by attending Toastmasters groups.

Don't wait to be inspired. If you want to build your business by speaking, stop talking about it. Just do it. Figure out what steps you can take right now, and do something to move forward.

However you do it, just do it. Get on as many stages as you can and watch your business thrive.

❋ ❋ ❋

Toni Caruso has over 30 years of event production experience during which she managed and successfully organized large and small events for the entertainment, corporate, and business-to-business worlds. Using her skills, experience, and behind-the-scenes event knowledge, she helps professionals educate, inform, and share their genius live on stage. In the speaking world she guides, teaches, and helps speakers, experts, and gifted messengers stand out and monetize their message. Using the techniques Toni teaches, her clients use speaking to quickly build their business, showcase their expertise and create breakthrough results. Toni is a wife and Army mom, and a staunch supporter of our military worldwide.

www.academy4speakers.com

Your Circumstances Don't Dictate Your Future

Justine Chomski

The dark days I've been through have given me the strength and ability to handle almost every situation that comes my way. I don't always appreciate how much of a skill that is. My mindset is that there's really nothing I need to fear because I have the knowledge and the experience to handle it. I know how to pull myself out of those dark days because I've done it before.

Life didn't turn out the way my husband and I planned. We had to accept that we were never going to be able to have children. My hormone journey started when we were trying to conceive. We got wrapped up in the fertility-clinic route. I had to take all these drugs and give myself injections. But the drugs were so hard on my system. I never had experienced severe PMS or mood swings and irritability before. When those infertility drugs started making me feel like I was crazy, I realized what other women experience.

I can remember the exact moment I thought, *I'm done. I'm done. Can't do this anymore.* Thankfully, my husband and I put our relationship and my mental health first, and I stopped all drugs without going the full IVF route

It took us time to mourn the life we thought we were going to have, but we have settled into this beautiful life together without children and cherish the relationship we have. If I were to get pregnant now, I wouldn't know what to do. Our life is more blessed than I ever imagined. We have two elderly dogs. We've traveled the world. And we have great relationships with our nieces and nephews.

We look for other ways to connect with children. We donate to a foundation for children. When we travel to other countries, we visit schools. I've even taught yoga to kids. In Nicaragua, we volunteered in a community that had faced a natural disaster. We made meals for the families and played with the children. They have very little, and yet these kids are so happy, so joyful, and so grateful. Our volunteer work brings so much joy to us and warms our hearts.

Sure, I've had trauma, and I have bad days, but I don't let those keep me down. I've had all the fun stuff to go along with all that. Therapy is another tool that helps me look at the life that I've been given, with all its challenges, and find myself in gratitude for the really beautiful moments.

The tough times we all go through shape us—they don't define the rest of our lives. I don't let my challenges be my story. I refuse to allow myself to dwell in that victim state. Without the struggles I've had, I definitely would not be where I am today, and I would not be pushing limits every day.

I have friends and relatives that have been given a silver spoon their whole life, and they don't know how to handle adversity. My challenges have taught me how be resilient and to roll with the punches.

You're resilient too. Don't let fear stop you. Spend some time thinking about how your life could be if you did the things that you want to do, rather than not doing things because you're fearful.

Even during this pandemic and lockdowns, there are people who are moving forward and finding new opportunities. Other people are sitting around waiting for things to go back to normal. It will not go back to normal. Let's accept that and step into our new reality. For me, that's the reality of a life without children of my own.

We're all scared to face the unknown. But the scariest thing is continuing to play small. Step forward. Don't worry about making mistakes. None of us is perfect. You won't know what you can do until you try. Every time I host an event, I have those butterflies: *What am I doing? Why am I doing this?* Every time I get ready to step on the stage, I don't want to talk—but I do it. And I grow from every experience.

Women who push the limits don't let fear set in. We step forward. We jump off that ledge. If we crash and burn, we have a harness that we can rely on—our experience and our mindset—to helps us find our way back.

It's not your circumstances that dictate your future. Create a mindset that is so powerful and a dream that is so big that you keep on going and pushing the limits of your amazing life.

❋ ❋ ❋

Justine Chomski is a successful entrepreneur who has owned numerous businesses, mainly in health and wellness. She has worked as a yoga instructor, nutritional therapist, Ayurveda practitioner, and event planner. Her interest in marketing and her experience building her own businesses led her to teach female health and wellness entrepreneurs how to increase their online visibility. She provides proven strategies and services that get more eyes on her clients' businesses. Her done-for-you services include designing websites, marketing funnels, summits, and virtual events. Justine has worked with companies like Smirnoff and Pepsi, as well as several sports celebrities.

www.prepareplanlaunch.com
Instagram: justinechomskimacdonald

Faith is an Action Word

Natalie Clayton

You can say, *I believe, I believe, I believe*, but if you don't put those words into action, your beliefs are useless. Faith is an action word.

I look at everything that happens in my life—the good and the bad—and know it's all a learning process. My mindset and my faith get me through whatever I encounter.

I was so excited when I was sworn in as a peace officer to represent the State of California, to help people, to work in the community, and to carry a gun. I wanted to use my 30-plus years of life experience to serve. Thinking that would be the toughest thing I'd have to go through, I said to myself, *If I can get through this paramilitary police academy training, I can get through anything.* I was wrong about it being the toughest thing, but I was right about getting through anything.

When my 22-year-old son was hit and dragged 300 yards by a bus, he was not expected to live. Every day was touch and go as he underwent surgery after surgery, sometimes three in a week. Day after day, as I sat by his bedside, I opened my Bible and prayed, *Okay Lord, I trust you. Your word is a breath of life.* I felt the presence of God. I chose to believe God is a healer and that he was present with me and my son every day of those 10 terrible months in the hospital. My faith and my trust in God held me up during that agonizing time. And, with the grace of God, my son survived.

The next year, my marriage fell apart. Getting a divorce was a shock, but I realized later it was a blessing in disguise.

Then, the same year, with no warning, I was diagnosed with the C word—cancer. I used what I learned from my son's situation and put my faith into action. I was proactive about my healing. I did research. In addition to consulting an oncologist, I went to a holistic practitioner. I wanted to be healed. I wanted to survive.

Chemo started three months after I had surgery. My oncologist told me not to go to the gym. To me, doing everything that doctor told me to do meant I believed I was sick. Instead, I went to the gym every day. I prayed every day and envisioned myself completely healed. I believed it. I was healed. That was eight years ago and I'm still healthy.

Faith and healing start in your mind. I chose to believe and trust God. I'm not saying that I was okay every day. It was challenging. Yet **every day** I made the decision to survive, and I took action on that belief.

My lifelong walk with God prepared me to get through those three major challenges all within a couple of years. I got through because of my mindset, my belief in who I am, and my faith in God. As you can imagine, there was a lot of prayer involved in it all: *I have faith in God. I have faith in myself. I'm going to get over this. I'm going to be healed and move past this.* I felt this inner strength and power continue to grow.

Your mind controls everything in your body. You can overcome anything in your life no matter what it is. That doesn't mean that you're not going to go through valleys and peaks and deserts and challenges. But in order to get to the mountain tops, you have to go through some valleys.

Getting through the valleys starts with your mind and your faith. You make that decision, that choice, and that commitment to yourself and whatever your higher source is for you. Then you tap into that faith and take action.

❄ ❄ ❄

Natalie J Clayton is an award-winning speaker, educator, certified life-transformation coach, and sought-after self-change strategist. She is the founder of TILT Synergy, Inc. and Life Revitalization Strategies, where she shares her astute insights to help others rise up to a better way to live. Her education includes a Bachelor of Arts in public administration, and a Master of Science in human services, organizational management, and leadership. Among other professional highlights, Natalie excelled as a police officer, parole agent, and law enforcement professor, amassing over twenty years of experience in all aspects of police training including investigations, crime prevention, trauma assessment, and even undercover. Her life has been all about standing strong in her power, optimizing adversity, and making a positive difference in the world, whether she was defying the school bully, refusing to let cruel insults deter her from securing the win for her sports team, or insisting on her right to an unprejudiced and harassment-free workplace during her time with the Department of Justice. She embodies her professional catchphrase, "Brilliance by Belief."

www.tiltsynerginc.com

Zip on a Different Character

Julie Cotton

I've been blessed to have technology skills that I combine with acting and improv techniques as a way to explore who I am and what I'm capable of. I use this knowledge both on and offstage.

In my life quest to know myself, I give myself permission to play with lots of different characters. I love to experiment with a character and traits that aren't me and see how those traits can serve me.

During a meditation, I got a "download" for an improv comedy card game. This game came in fully developed: *Here you go, do this*. I felt like a steward of the information. And within two weeks, I had a prototype copy of that game. Then I needed to find the capital to pull the trigger and produce it. Ultimately, I went on a 30-city national tour and put it out on social media. That felt fun.

The difficult part for me was putting myself out there and asking other people for money for a thing that I love to do and would do for free if I could. In order to make this happen, I had to find my *I'm-Great-at-Sales* character and let her ask people for money.

In improv, we learn how to step into the shoes of another character in an instant. We get to access any character we want, and we can change characters moment to moment to moment. So, if a scene isn't going well, we can literally turn around and create a new character in a new scene.

Imagine that you have a closet full of attributes—

characters—that you can choose from at any moment to serve the scene you're in. Just grab that costume, step into it, and zip it up.

When I zip up the costume of this other persona that's not me, everything is still going to come through my actor's instrument, through my body, through my voice, through my imagination. I get to try on totally different characters by zipping up a different costume. I can choose to be this grumpy, quirky person. But it's not me, so it's okay. If people judge the character, they're not really judging me. And when I'm through with that character for the moment, I unzip that costume, put it back in the closet, and I'm still me.

This frees me to try new things without judgement, offstage as well as onstage.

In my day-to-day life, when I feel like I'm not successful or confident, I zip on a successful, confident character's costume. For example, like many of us during the pandemic, I've been sitting at a computer a lot lately. I used to have a story in my mind that *I'm not good with technical things*. But that's just a character. So, when I hit a snag with technology, I say to myself: *Well, let's not let **that** character handle this right now. We're just going to put that one over there. I'm calling forth the character that **is** good at tech, or at least is willing to have the beginner's mind to learn how to be good at tech.* That shifts my focus and gives me confidence that I will get through the tech challenge, no matter what.

Zipping on a different character serves the scene, whatever is going on at the time. I look at what is needed in the moment and zip on the appropriate character.

This approach shows up when I'm coaching clients. I find out how people respond—what kind of a coach they actually need. Some people need a cheerleader, someone to tell them: *You're doing amazing. Keep going. You're awesome.* Somebody else might need a drill sergeant: *Hey, get down and give me 20. Go! No more playing around. Let's get it done.* I am neither a cheerleader nor a drill sergeant. I do however, have access to both characters and can zip up whichever one serves that client.

I worked with a very accomplished mathematician who was working on her graduate level degree at Rutgers, the only woman in her department. She was responsible for teaching undergraduate courses but had never been taught how to teach. **Teaching** the material is a completely different skill than **knowing** it. She wanted to build her confidence in teaching.

Using acting skills, she learned to put on the persona of a math professor: a character that is resourceful and confident, who can stand in front of a classroom with authority and competence, and who can expertly teach the material she knows. She gave herself permission to metaphorically zip up the costume of her mathematical professor anytime she *stepped on stage* in her classroom.

Decide on a few characters to have readily available and develop those characters ahead of time. It might be passion or playfulness or confidence or courage. Flesh out each character and play with it. Discover how you would be if you had those characteristics.

Give yourself permission to zip yourself into any one of those characters and call up the attributes you need for whatever scene is playing in your life at the moment.

❋ ❋ ❋

Julie Cotton, an Arizona native, has been an actor and improviser for nearly four decades, and a wellness practitioner since 2007. She is the founder and CEO of Next Level Improv where she empowers individuals and teams by training them in improv techniques. She is an avid student of life with lots of letters and certificates: MFA in acting, BA in theater education, licensed massage therapist, Pilates and yoga instructor, second-degree black belt in kickboxing, and transformational trainer. She is a bestselling author and the inventor of an interactive improv card game.

www.nextlevelimprov.com

Choose to Be Happy

Staci Danford

You are in charge of your own happiness. You have it right there inside you. Regardless of what's going on outside you, the one place you do have control is within your brain. You may not have control of your house, your car, your kids, your spouse, or your job. But you've got control over your brain. With your brain, you can do anything.

I come from a long line of addiction. Everybody on my dad's side of the family is an addict—an alcoholic, a drug addict. My brother died of a drug overdose. I had lots of hurt as a kid, yet I choose to be happy.

To be happy, you don't have to have everything go great in your life. That's what my whole goal is to tell people. You don't have to be born with a lot of money, or live in a four-bedroom, three-bath house, and drive a car that's paid for. You can be happy regardless of your life circumstances.

Some of the greatest research comes from Holocaust victims who have taught us the most about gratitude. In grad school, several of my classmates and I did a research study where we read Holocaust stories and examined the mindsets of those who faced unthinkable tragedy. Many of these survivors were thankful for what we might normally see as small things, like the man that stuffed breadcrumbs under the fence, or another who brought them a jacket, for example.

I asked myself: *Staci, if they can find gratitude during the Holocaust, who are you to not be grateful? Find something, girl. Get up and look for it. If it's only to look out the window and reflect that I don't live in a war zone. I am safe, with a roof over my head and food to eat. I have clean water to drink. Thousands and thousands of people do not even have that.*

If people can overcome the Holocaust, we can do anything we want.

We don't think about what we have until it's taken away from us—just like my brother. I miss him every day. He's been dead nearly 20 years. But instead of focusing on the one day of his death, I have chosen to focus on the 32 years of his life. I still love him, and I pretend he's here in my head. In every family picture, right before we took it, he would stick his finger in my ear. I remember the goofy things like that, and that he loved my children like they were his own. And I can instantly smile as I think of him instead of feeling sad that he's not here anymore.

These are choices that I make every day, choices that you can make too. Push yourself to get out of your negativity and find something, anything, that you're grateful for.

There are homeless people who are grateful. There are millionaires who are grateful. There are millionaires who are miserable. And it's not about the money.

My favorite research study is from David Steindl-Rast, a 94-year-old Benedictine monk who speaks about gratitude. He says that we think that it's happy people who are grateful, but it's not. **It is grateful people who are happy.** All of the research will back that up.

Regardless of where you are in your life, how much money you have, what job you have, what relationships you have, **you can be happy when you choose to be grateful**.

❋ ❋ ❋

Staci Danford is a speaker and educational neuroscientist. Her master's degree is in mind/brain education with a focus on the neuroscience of gratitude and the impact of gratitude on the brain. She is the owner and operator of The Grateful Brain, a consulting company that works with individuals and companies to increase their overall wellbeing. She has 25 years of teaching and communication experience and was voted one of the top 10 teachers of 2016 by *Fort Worth Magazine*. She has educated thousands of people how using their brain to maximize their strengths helps them achieve greater success. Staci's greatest desire is to help people believe in their own greatness and work together to change the world.

www.thegratefulbrain.com

Trust Budget

Linsey Dyer

Even after my trust was shattered early in my life, I have made a conscious choice to start every relationship with a *positive trust budget*. With everyone I meet, I start out trusting them and believing they are trustworthy. Everyone. And it's up to them to accept that trust or to erode it.

Most people really don't trust others. The decision to trust is not easy for everyone, and it's a choice each person makes consciously or subconsciously. Going out on a limb and trusting someone is a precursor to being able to love them. If you don't trust them, you're not going to love them. Maybe it works both ways—that love and trust work together. Maybe love can crack through the ice of distrust and melt it.

Trust has to start with trusting yourself first. Trust your gut reaction. Trust the intuition that tells you something's wrong even though this person, or this job opportunity, or this move, or this whatever it happens to be, looks perfect on paper. You've got to trust yourself to know what is best for you, to trust your intuition. We intuitively know whether we're in relationships which are good for us or not. We start out by trusting this person, but then trust ourselves enough to say, *Yes, this is working,* or *No, it's not,* and get the heck out of there.

I learned to hone and trust my instincts at a very early age.

When I was eight years old, after I watched my father bully a little boy I'd been playing with, I made a mental note that there was something not right about him. I realized that he was a dreadful person who couldn't be trusted. That was my first lesson: Just because someone is an adult, doesn't mean you have to trust them.

My mother taught me that accountability is a critical component of trust. She taught me to examine: *What am I accountable for? What am I not accountable for? What is under my control and what is not under my control?*

Empowerment came from clearly knowing: *This is not my fault. This has nothing to do with me. There's something wrong in my father's head.* I suffered no illusions. My ability to see the wound in my oppressor is a gift that has served me well. I was lucky that I realized it was him I couldn't trust, not myself.

I've had many opportunities to practice that important lesson, not only during my childhood when my father became frightening to live with, but in my education and business as well. That knowledge has been invaluable.

I was one of six women out of two hundred students in the electrical engineering program at university. At the end of the first year, a couple of other girls and I were studying for our lab exam. A tall, athletic tutor asked, "Why are you girls here anyway?" Our bemused reply was, "What do you mean? We're practicing for the exam." He actually said, "Yeah, but why are you in electrical engineering? You're girls!" It was such a jarring and irritating question. But because I'd learned to distinguish whether something had to do with me or not, I didn't take it as discouraging. I just told myself, *Something's wrong with this guy.* I knew it was his problem and not mine.

Because I trust myself, I know I'm safe to choose to start every relationship with that positive trust budget.

With my positive trust budget and awareness of accountability, I had the confidence I needed to enter a field comprised mostly of men. I have spent decades as an engineer and love mentoring young women who want to navigate business dynamics and push the limits in their careers. Young women are inspiring, and they're clever, and they're good, and they're multi-capable. And, they're just fun.

Here's the advice I offer them—and you.

First things first, **get yourself a network**. Get yourself a cohort of supporters. Get yourself a group who will encourage and help you, who see you, who share in your vision of your success, and who will support your vision. They don't have to be in your company or from your class. They don't have to be in your age group. Just surround yourself with people who will help you to see yourself better and to see your potential.

Look for a mentor. A mentorship relationship should work both ways. A good, strong, mentor relationship is one where both the mentor and the mentee get value out of it. Don't be afraid to gently fire a mentor if the mentor doesn't fit. Keep looking until you find the relationship that works.

Be your own praise singer. Other people will pick up on that. It's very hard for women to be their own praise singers. We are not socialized to say to others, or even to ourselves: "I'm good at this. I did this well." We're socialized to be modest. So, the trick is to get your coven, your support group, to be your praise singers with you and for you.

Whether you're in a non-traditional role or a more traditional one, **find time to be with yourself**, and to ground yourself in who you are and who you believe you can be. Focus on being rather than doing. We tend to get so caught up in operational tasks, especially when we're starting out in our careers. *I need to do this. I need to accomplish that. I need to get this registration. I need to get this certificate. I need to take that course. I need to get that qualification.* That's all doing. Love yourself. And find ways to focus on who you are and how to become even more of who you want to be.

✳ ✳ ✳

Linsey Dyer is a civil engineer, entrepreneur, innovative business leader, and stepmom. She was born in England, lived in Canada for 30 years, and has now lived in South Africa for over 24 years. She is the co-founder and executive director of ENDEVA Limited, which develops infrastructure assets to provide clean energy solutions to small private commercial clients, initially in Zambia. She has worked on three continents in 41 countries, 34 of which are in Africa. Linsey has more than three decades of experience in multinational companies, including her own, with a deep focus in the energy sector. She is passionate about doing good business through sustainable infrastructure business cases and good governance, as well as contributing to nation-building in South Africa. She enjoys volunteering where she can have a tangible impact, including mentoring young women in Science, Technology, Engineering and Math (STEM), leading and supporting business chambers, and most recently, as the chairwoman of the local residents' association, a non-profit with over 2,000 members in a community of about 14,000. Linsey summited Mt. Kilimanjaro in August 2009 with a group of extraordinary women (and some amazing men) and has since used that experience as inspiration for approaching many different challenges…including living through her partner Tim's terminal cancer.

www.endevasolutions.com
www.6thwaveafrica.com

Be Fearless—Make Mistakes

Sarah Fuentes

I've spent my lifetime dancing with other people's expectations. My family, my classmates, my teachers and professors—they all expected me to dance to a different rhythm. Sorting out my own unique dance has been challenging.

I read and wrote from age three, and always excelled in school. My teachers loved me. Every time there was a National Geographic Bee or a poetry contest, I was the one nominated and would bring home trophies and certificates. I was in a gifted and talented program by seventh grade but adjusting to college was tough.

My parents couldn't afford to send me to the fantastic East Coast colleges that accepted me: Brown, NYU, Cornell. So, I got a scholarship to a small, liberal arts college in Minnesota, with less than a hundred people of color, where I was one of only two Puerto Ricans. It was a world away from my Bronx home.

For the first time, I felt judged for my race and culture. People didn't think I was smart because of my baggy clothes and how I carried myself. They heard my very thick New York accent and judged that I was a certain type. A lot of international students would say, "Oh, we don't hang out with the American students of color. All they want to do is party; they're not here to study. You'll mess up our GPAs." Their families had warned them about "our type."

My high school classes had been engaging and progressive, not lecture style. Now, in college, I was reading pages and pages in textbooks and sitting in long lectures with no interaction. That's not the way I learn.

My science teachers sent me notes when my scores were poor: "This is hard for people like you. This is probably the first time you're getting work like this." Or people would say, "You are here on scholarship, aren't you?" It was so unjust.

When my grades dropped and I was expelled in my sophomore year, it was a shock. For a while, I wallowed in self-pity. I threw myself a pity party. *Oh my god, this was so hard, and I've suffered so much.* I rebelled, and I made some poor decisions, one of which led to an unwanted pregnancy.

I had failed for the first time ever at anything and had to move back home. I kept the pregnancy a secret from my parents because I felt like that was just too much of a disappointment. I stayed in bed for days, not knowing what to do.

I soon went to therapy where my counselors explained that my experience wasn't new. Difficulties arise for many bright and gifted students of color when they experience failure for the first time and are not sure how to handle all the social changes. Wow! That **is** what happened to me. It contextualized everything for me.

I took a loan and attended classes at a local public college. Because I couldn't afford books, I spent long hours every night at the library, reading as much as I could and taking notes.

My professor in a woman's studies course noticed my work and my demeanor, and she challenged me. "What's going on with you? I see your papers, so I know what you are capable of. But you sit in class and you're just not there. Something's wrong." When I finished telling her everything, she said, "And? Do you think you're the first woman to ever be in this situation? Do you think you're the first woman who was ever judged and diminished in that way? Do you think you're the first woman who ever found herself pregnant and not ready? No, you're not. You're not the first and you're not the last. You can sit here and sulk. Or you can do something about it. So, what are you going to do?"

I didn't get her sympathy or a shoulder to cry on, but her kick in the butt helped me realize it was time for me to forgive myself for failing and move on.

I needed to be on my own, to try things out, and do things differently. And to make mistakes. I needed to take a risk and go back to college in Minnesota. I got an abortion. I reapplied to school. I was accepted back my junior year. I even graduated on time.

Real feelings are part of the experience. Feeling your feelings and owning your stuff is painful. Guilt is only going to hold you back and stop your progress. When you forgive yourself, you can roll past it and figure out what to do next.

It's not easy. Therapy can help. It helped me.

In order to push your limits, first consider what those limits are. Are they limits someone else has put upon you? If so, acknowledge that those limits do not define you. Convince yourself that they don't exist. Know that you can push past them. Then make the choice and take action to push past whatever limits you perceive.

Be fearless as you push forward. You will make mistakes— we all make mistakes. That's okay. That's part of growing. We've all been through tough times and have survived. You will survive.

Forgive yourself when you make mistakes. Don't judge yourself and don't let others judge you. When I messed up again at school, my friends told me it wasn't a big deal—we all mess up. That's the attitude to hold on to so you can move ahead.

Fearlessly try different things and figure out what brings you joy. Find ways to connect with others and bring joy to them too. You're stepping on stones of your past mistakes and challenges and building on them to create a more beautiful way to live.

❋ ❋ ❋

Sarah Fuentes is an educator and entrepreneur with a bachelor's degree in anthropology, and two master's degrees, one in education and one in mathematics and leadership. From the time she was three years old, she was reading and writing. As a classroom teacher for 15 years, she worked hard to give her students a quality education and create new leaders who are risk-takers and independent thinkers, not robots. Realizing there are two education systems—one for the haves and one for the have-nots—she moved into school leadership to help create the kind of school where all students receive a quality education. As an instructional coach, Sarah helps teachers create strong relationships with students. She embraces her role as a political activist educator and disruptor. She has created and produces Math Mini-Lessons, an online curriculum that helps students build a strong foundation in math by providing quality lessons and engages students in investigating concepts and building new habits.

www.mathminilessons.com
Facebook: Math Mini-Lessons

Find Your Purpose

Whitedove Gannon

Every single person has a purpose in their life, and we are all meant to make a conscious choice to live into that purpose. But how do you discover it? Actually, we already have the answers we need. The problem is we don't trust our innate ability to allow those answers to come out and serve us. We may need guidance, but we do have the answers. And we do have a calling. And we **do** have a purpose.

When my husband and I decided we were ready for a less stressful life, we sold our construction business in Colorado and moved away from families, friends, and everything that was normal to us. We fantasized about a great adventure as we created a 160-acre sustainable farm in Kansas. We loved the idea of coexisting with the animals, the land, and the ecosystem in a symbiotic relationship. We thought our three kids—and the one on the way—would enjoy a simpler life living off the land.

We knew nothing about Kansas, and even worse, we knew nothing about sustainable farming. The model was not at all popular in southeast Kansas, the heart of conventional farm country. For us, it was about creating a movement, taking the risk of not being understood, and discovering what was possible. We were quite the oddballs.

After almost five years, I realized our venture wasn't meant to last any longer. One day I just knew it was time to go back to

Denver. My husband told me, "Sleep it off. You're tired. You'll wake up tomorrow and everything will be fine." But this was different. It's weird. It came to me suddenly in the form of a strong, strong pull.

It's easy to disregard those feelings. But if we're honest about the calling itself, with who we are, with what we were meant to do, and what our purpose is in this world, then we know to honor that pull toward our purpose. We don't worry about how it might look to the outside world. When we accept it and allow it to be present, we're able to shift and move in that direction. We know that it is time and know that this is now the direction of our path.

Everything had brought me to that point. I needed to move forward from there.

This pull is an internal thing. It's being true to yourself. It's ultimately finding the purpose that you are called for. It's allowing that to be your motivator and your driving force. It's less about the external benchmarks or accolades or the external things that signify that you are successful.

I was successful. Plenty of people told me we were quitting the farm venture too soon, that we were ready to break out and be extremely lucrative. But it wasn't about being lucrative. It was about doing what I was called to do. It was about purpose.

Now, years later, there are several sustainable farms in that area of Kansas. This movement brought in a wave of new people and new ideas. I didn't create that atmosphere. But my willingness to do something that other people weren't doing paved the way for it. I broke the ice. I showed people it could be done. I fulfilled that purpose.

When we moved out to Kansas to start the farm, the calling was just as clear as when it was time to be over. Both were steps I needed to take at the time. And I believe what we accomplished was needed for that community. After five years, I did what I was meant to do, and I learned what I was meant to learn. I took the lessons I learned, peeled back layers of myself, and moved forward on my path.

It's a process to learn to lean in and listen to your intuition. It doesn't come by just thinking, *Okay, now I'm going to let the internal piece be my driving factor.* It's about evolving as a human. It takes time. I still get stuck in my head, but I am able to recognize when I do and move forward through it.

You must be willing to allow these answers to come up. When things get tight or uneasy, step back and notice what's going on in the moment. Because we easily get distracted by the day-to-day chores of life, learning to be in the moment is extremely critical. Be present. Listen internally. Make a conscious choice in whatever you do to show up authentically, aware, and ready to bring value.

Set your goal, but don't overthink the end result. Realize that once you start on that path, you **will** get there. We want so badly for there to be a straight line to get us there. But it's not going to be a straight line at all. Let the journey be more about what it **is**, and less about what you want to make it.

In order to stay grounded and connect with your purpose, give yourself quiet time daily to pray or meditate.

Journaling is the way to start opening the door to your subconscious so you can see the thoughts and underlying beliefs that are holding you back. You may think, *I already know these things. They're in my head.* They may be in your head, but you haven't examined them, and they're not moving you forward.

Go back later with an open mind and think about what you've written down.

When you crack the door open, it will naturally start allowing more awareness and inner wisdom to come up. Once that's in your conscious mind, you'll be able to address your thoughts, beliefs, and contradictions. You'll be inspired by the trajectory of your growth as you find your purpose.

❋ ❋ ❋

Whitedove Gannon, the founder and creator of the Female Entrepreneur Movement and the Scaling CEO Method, is a business growth strategist. She partners with successful women entrepreneurs using her Scaling CEO Method to dial in their systems and operations and scale to seven figures and beyond. She has been a trusted advisor and trainer for Pete Vargas as well as Dean Graziosi, coaching hundreds of entrepreneurs in their scaling programs. With 20-plus years of entrepreneurial success under her belt, including running a construction company and a sustainable farm, Whitedove is on a mission to help women business owners scale faster while making the impact they desire. These days, you'll find her enjoying time with her husband and five children or relaxing and enjoying a good business book in the beautiful mountains of Colorado.

www.g7creativeagency.com
www.whitedove-gannon.com
www.whitedove-gannon.com/podcast

Build Your Support Network

Haley Gray

There's an African proverb that says, *Alone, you'll go fast. Together, you'll go far.* From experience, I know how important it is to not try to do it alone, whether it's in your personal life or your business.

One of the most important things you can do to ensure your success is to build a support network for yourself and create a board of advisors for your business.

While I was finishing my MBA and working my way up the leadership ladder in the company that I worked for, I was taking care of my dad who needed full-time care as well as raising four children between the ages of four and 12. It was a huge challenge.

I was shocked to see how few women were in leadership positions, especially in STEM fields. At the time—and I'm talking fairly recently: 2011 to 2012—only about ten percent of the students in my class were women.

I really saw how many women didn't have the support, mentoring, and infrastructure they needed to allow them to be successful, get a promotion, or achieve their leadership goals. How can you if you're stretched to that hairy, ragged edge?

So many times we're doing what we have to each day, just putting one foot in front of the other. We're getting kids to daycare, working all day, fetching kids, feeding them, getting them to bed, crashing. And then getting up the next day to lather, rinse, and repeat. Heaven forbid the kids get sick. There's no time to get out of the weeds long enough to plan a career or start a business.

My secret to having a family and running a business is having an exceptional support network. I wouldn't be where I am now without assistance from my spouse, phenomenal childcare, and the support community around me. I couldn't have done it alone. I was fortunate enough to have *au pairs* until my children were older. Because of them, there were a lot of responsibilities that I simply didn't have to worry about.

I've also built friendships and a community that I can rely on. That takes time. People won't instantly offer to babysit your kids when they first meet you, especially not four at one time.

Five years ago, my daughter sustained a traumatic brain injury after a fall from a horse that resulted in severe psychiatric issues. I can't just hire somebody to babysit or take care of all her needs. Even in the best circumstances, it takes me 20 hours a week just to manage her care. The ability to hire help has vanished.

Coping with this situation with our oldest child while managing the three younger ones has not been easy. The support network that I've built over the years has helped me get through. I wave the white flag and put word out into the community when I don't know what to do.

I've given a ton to others, and it comes back to me when I need it. People have stepped forward and offered me information, advice, and resources. They've helped find an attorney to work through the disability process, and a social worker who made recommendations about group homes. Sometimes it's just little nuggets of information here and there. But when I put it all together, it's enough that I've been able to work my way through the system without having to get lost in the weeds.

Even though the last few years have been incredibly difficult because of the extent of my daughter's issues, I'm so grateful that I've had support and flexibility that has enabled us to manage and cope with life.

In addition to having a support system in my personal life, I've built relationships and an indispensable support system around my business.

Whether you're in a corporate job or own your own business, formal and informal mentorship is vitally important—maybe even more so if you're a small business owner. But finding the right people takes time and careful attention.

Because I'm an introvert, it's sometimes super scary to go to networking meetings or to schedule a one-on-one with people. Being an engineer and an MBA doesn't exactly scream "extrovert."

Knowing that you never build anything great by staying in your comfort zone, I've had to get out of my comfort zone to build my support structure.

I have cultivated a tremendous board of advisors for my business, primarily women, who have a depth of experience and perspective that is invaluable to me. These people are honestly much brighter than I am at certain things. They're people that love me enough to tell me "no." And they call me on my BS. I appreciate that they'll give me a hard time—not in a mean way— but to help me grow as a business owner and as a leader.

To find the right people, carefully set your intentions of connecting with people who share your values and will serve your business. Decide very specifically what you're looking for.

When I was looking for a financial person to help me with accounting and somebody to help me with legal matters, I knew exactly the kind of people I wanted and what I expected them to do. It's amazing how they materialized once I set well-defined intentions and started connecting with people. It's cool to see it all come together, and to see the right people show up when you begin with the end in mind.

At the end of the day, it's about people and relationships. It's in those relationships with other people that the success happens in your business and your life. Create your support team. Then see how far you can go together.

❊ ❊ ❊

Haley Lynn Gray is a bestselling author, speaker, coach, and marketing wizard who fixes broken websites for fun. She founded the *Leadership Girl* blog in 2012 with the radical notion that women can harness their unique power and skills to become highly effective leaders. Her studies for her MBA from Duke's Fuqua School of Business concentrated on entrepreneurship and innovation. Through her company, In2itive Biz Solutions, she focuses on helping small business owners with their business and marketing strategies. Haley is the mother of four active kids who have their own mini zoo in their home. Look for her bestselling books *Leadership Girl* and *Fearless Marketing*. Women's Entrepreneur Network, the Facebook networking and support group Haley created, has quickly grown to a community of over 75,000 thriving entrepreneurs. She'd love for you to join.

www.in2itivebiz.com
www.facebook.com/groups/WomensEntrepreneurNetwork/

"I Didn't Raise You to be a Quitter"

Diana Gregory

When I graduated from college in the '70s and started my marketing career at Anheuser-Busch, there were very few women in that male-dominated beer business. Those were times when women didn't even think there was a glass ceiling that could be broken. Thirty years later when I left my last position there, I was still the only woman in the company who had held my executive position. Changes were slow.

Six months after I started my first position, my supervisor said, right to my face, "Women have no place in the beer business." I was petrified. *Well, what do I do? Do I call HR, or just what?*

My mother's voice echoed in my mind: "I didn't raise you to be a quitter." So, I told myself, *I'll show him. I will just work harder and get promoted. Then I'll work for another boss who may have more appreciation for the wonderful work that women are contributing here.*

I continued to work, and work, and work. After a year, I was promoted and started moving up in the company. I didn't let negativity get in the way of what I was trying to achieve, and I didn't quit.

Twenty years later the supervisor who thought women didn't

belong in the beer business was starting up a new department and was looking for directors. He put the word out, "I really want Diana Gregory on my team." I worked in that position for six months and then I was promoted. I proved myself to him and to others in the company. I never gave up on any of the positions I had.

I was often the only woman on a team, and I felt excluded many times. But I never let it bother me—or at least I didn't let it show. Sometimes after a meeting, the team would all go skiing. Afterward, all the guys would get in the hot tub and smoke cigars. That's something that I would not do. That's not me. I just got used to things being the way they were.

I was sales director one year when our team won a competition for a trip to Pebble Beach. One of the guys said, "Why is Diana Gregory going? She can't even hit a golf ball." I didn't get upset. I took him aside and told him this incentive contest was all about promoting the team. It was about abundance—there's enough for everyone. But he had a mindset of scarcity—"me, myself, and I." He really missed the point.

It just so happens I did play golf. So, I told him, "Come on outside and bring your irons and your woods. We'll see who can hit a golf ball." I heard the guys laughing. "I've got my money on Diana." He got what I was saying. After that he showed a lot more respect for me.

It was a teaching moment. And I never missed an opportunity to educate the guys.

When I was assigned an account in downstate Illinois, one of the guys said, in a phony southern accent, "We wuz real worried 'bout her comin' down here, bein' Black an' bein' a woman. But they reeeelly like her." With a smile, I drawled, "Why thank yew veery much."

My coworkers were so surprised to discover that one of my customers and his wife invited me to their home for dinner. My male coworkers were not expecting that kind of response to a

Black woman who was asking business owners to sell our beer. It meant a lot to me that customers were willing to open their homes up to me. This couple, and other customers too, are still friends of mine more than 30 years later.

During my career at Anheuser-Busch there were a lot of things I dealt with that gave me the opportunity to prove to my mother—and myself—that I am NOT a quitter.

I have a strong faith to fall back on. When things were tough and I felt disappointed, I always prayed for guidance.

In addition to my faith, the strong values and principles my parents had instilled in me were my guide: always work hard, give everything my best effort, don't let negativity get in the way, don't take it personally, and stick with it. Those principles have driven me all my life. In giving my best effort, sometimes I had to work on something a little longer. In the end though, that always paid off. I learned to develop endurance and a thick skin no matter what I encountered. I got used to things as they were and learned not to take things personally. I learned how to be a professional and gained the skills I needed to build strong, lasting relationships and deal with anyone—from a customer to a coworker, and from a boss to a team member.

I found that I am a much better person—a much stronger person—because I accepted challenges, pushed the limits, and didn't quit.

❋ ❋ ❋

Diana Gregory grew up in the housing projects in St. Louis, Missouri, graduated valedictorian of her class, earned a degree from Boston University through a full scholarship, and enjoyed a successful thirty-year, multifaceted corporate marketing and sales career with Anheuser-Busch. She excelled at a time when it was uncommon for women to even have a career in the beer industry. In 2009, she began her encore career in Phoenix, Arizona by founding the Diana Gregory Outreach Services Foundation and operating her non-profit, Gregory's Fresh Market. She has positioned her marketing and sales expertise alongside her vision to drive positive, long-lasting change in the community by bringing her farmer's market delivery program to senior and veteran's facilities in Maricopa County. Diana and her volunteers teach healthy cooking, nutrition, and fitness education to those they serve. In 2021, her organization provided over 15,000 seniors and veterans with free bags of fresh fruit and vegetables. For decades, she has served on boards that advocate for minority opportunities and women, and her work on behalf of seniors has often been recognized. Diana has been making a difference *in* the community by giving back *to* the community. Every day she lives what her parents taught her: That it is not where you live, but what lives *in* you that determines where you will end up in life; and, to always live by an attitude of gratitude.

www.dianagregory.com

Say "YES" to as Many Opportunities as Possible

Erica Virvo Hackman

When I was growing up, I never wanted to travel. My parents signed me up for an overseas People to People trip three summers in a row. Every year they lost their deposit when, even though I'd agreed to go, at the last minute I told them I'd changed my mind. "I'm fine in Connecticut. I love it here. I'm okay. I don't want to travel."

Then when I was 20, everything changed. I realized I never wanted to be an interior designer, but instead of dropping out of college, I decided to complete my degree abroad. If I was going to stick it out, I'd finish it on an adventure. Transferring to my school's sister campus in Qatar changed my entire life and my view of the world.

I decided to experience Qatar to the fullest, so I created a rule that I had to say "yes" to everything unless it overlapped with something I had already committed to. What was the point of going to Qatar and sitting in my dorm room?

The new friends I made took me to the mall, to local restaurants, to their homes. We rode in a truck caravan into the desert where we raced through the sand dunes, played sand volleyball, and danced to loud music. It was such a quirky experience—everything was unexpected.

For five years after I graduated, I traveled to more than 40 countries—but not as a tourist. I spent time getting to know the people and finding out how they lived. I said "yes" to a lot of fascinating opportunities.

In Zambia, I lived in a termite clay hut and worked on a farming cooperative. Our village of 200 people had no running water or electricity. To shower, I'd go get water, make a fire, warm up the water, then dump a few bucketsful over my head.

In the Caribbean, I worked on a farm taking care of pigs and horses and donkeys. I walked through guava fields to get to the beach. With friends I made, I hitchhiked on the back of gravel trucks.

I taught English in Thailand and lived with a family in a town where nobody spoke English. While I was teaching English in South Korea, I dated a man who didn't speak English. We communicated by drawing pictures and reciting American rap lyrics.

I'm a terrible tourist. I am fine with never seeing the usual tourist sites or famous museums. Mostly, I sat in people's kitchens, cooking together and talking, and met their families. I even attended local weddings. No typical tourist experiences for me.

Since returning to New York City, I've worked for a travel blog. People come to me for travel advice. When I stop and think about it, I wonder, *How the heck did I get here?*

Nobody expected this young woman who grew up in suburban Connecticut and didn't like to travel to end up on so many adventures. But my travel adventures transformed me. They gave me a new perspective about the world and about people that I could never have realized if I'd stayed in Connecticut. I wholeheartedly believe that traveling makes friends of strangers, and the more friends there are in the world, the more peace there is in the world.

Everything you do makes you who you are. Even though I never ended up being an interior designer, I'm not unhappy that I went to interior design school. There would have never been a reason or an opportunity for me to go to our sister campus in Qatar if I hadn't been studying design at the time. And saying "yes" to that trip to Qatar started me on my journey.

When a new opportunity shows up, I don't need to have everything figured out before I say "yes." First, I put myself in the game. Once I make the decision to jump in, I figure it out. On-the-job training. Any internal conflict or fear seems to dissipate once I make that decision and take action on it. And the more I say "yes" to opportunities, the more confidence I develop that I can handle anything.

My life has taken so many twists and turns. I kept saying "yes" to things that sounded cool. I never imagined doing the things I did. But following the yeses, and following the things that felt good, gave me a deeper understanding of the world. And more importantly, a deeper understanding of myself.

✳ ✳ ✳

Erica Virvo Hackman is a purposeful traveler and connector who loves the thrill and challenge of living in places people have rarely heard of. At age 21, she chose to finish her last year of college on an adventure in Qatar. From that moment on, her life revolved around traveling cheaply with the money she earned from waitressing. She spent over five years studying, working, and farming in obscure countries in the Middle East, Asia, the Caribbean, and Africa. Now, Erica is the Director of *The Nomadic Network*, a travel community that organizes events for travel enthusiasts around the world. She teaches people how to bring their travel aspirations to life by exploring the world on a budget. She and her husband, Rich, recently welcomed their first child, and are thrilled to add the adventure of parenthood to their lives.

www.ourwholelifelove.com
www/nomadicmatt.com/travel-blogs/meet-the-team/

How Bad Do You Want It?

Terry Hardin

When you come up against challenges, ask yourself, *How bad do I want this?* Understand that when you say, *Whatever it takes,* you've got to mean it. Because it's completely possible that God is going to test you. You may get knocked down. You may get stomped and stepped on. That's when you have to decide if you are going to get up—or are you staying down?

There are tons of excuses you can tell yourself for staying down. *It's awful comfortable down here. I was a little warm, but the ground is nice and cool. I'll just sit here for a while.*

You don't have to pop up like a rabbit. Just get up, dust yourself off, and say to yourself, *Okay, that happened. Rejection letter number 185. All right. Now what? Do I still want to reach that goal? Yes, I do. Okay. Do I deserve it? Yes, I do.* Tell yourself you deserve it. Because you do. There's only one you. You're the only one who can do what you do the way you do it for the reasons you do it. Get started again.

Jim Rohn, a well-known author and motivational speaker, used to say, "You're human, not a goose. You don't suddenly find yourself flying to Florida because you **have** to fly south for the winter, thinking, *Oh my god, what happened? I really liked ice skating. I don't **want** to fly south for the winter.*" Take responsibility. You can't change the circumstances, but you can change yourself.

You can make your next day brand new if that's what you want. That's something only human beings can do. You, as a human being, are very special, very, very unique—and definitely the princess or prince of the universe. You can change your life.

So, ask yourself, *Do I want it?* Tell yourself, *I deserve it.* Then go get it. And if a dragon gets in your way—I happen to love dragons—but if a dragon or a wall or a nasty person shows up and dings you—because you will get your armor dinged—just wait. Heal a little bit and then ask yourself, *How can I get around this?* And if the challenge seems to be too much at the moment, take a breath, plant flowers, go to the ocean, or do whatever you do to relax. Then, when you come back to the challenge, you'll have a whole different perspective, and you can start fresh.

Next, act "as if," and tell those negative voices to calm down and be quiet. Understand, fear is going to try and get all over you. You're going to have a voice inside you that says, *Are you worthy?* Tell it to be quiet and go away!

When I speak to groups, my fee is five grand. At Akron University, when I was getting ready to step out onto the stage, all of a sudden, the voice inside my head said, *Are you **really** worth $5,000? What are you going to give people that's **really** worth $5,000? I mean, **really**?* And I had to say, *Voice, you need to shut up now. I'm about to go on stage.* Then I hitched up my boots and walked out onto the stage as if I were worth five grand. I looked at the people in the audience, and I loved on them. I said to myself, *They want to hear what I have to say, and I'm going to give them so much more than they expect.*

There are people out there whose whole purpose is to cut you down and make you stop. It's true, not everybody can be an actor, or an illustrator, or an Imagineer, or a TV talk show host. Not everybody can make it because they stopped partway—they stopped digging three feet from gold. But you can make it. You know you want it. You know you deserve it. Don't stop, keep digging.

Being the unique human being you are is the greatest gift in the world. Don't take it for granted. Be happy you're an adaptable human and not a goose. You're a magical human being. If today is not good, you can change it. You can live it differently tomorrow. Humans are amazing. Remember—that's you. That's what you are. And if you forget, call me and I'll remind you.

※ ※ ※

Terri Hardin is one of Walt Disney's legendary Imagineers. She has been with Disney since 1989 as a sculptor and concept artist helping design some of the most popular attractions for Disney parks in the United States, Paris, and Tokyo. For more than three decades, she has also been a puppeteer for the Jim Henson Company, creator of The Muppets. She worked in over 45 films and television shows including *Ghostbusters*, *Men in Black*, and *The Muppet Show.* Her private, limited edition Disney character sculpts include characters such as Remy, Stitch, Jiminy Cricket, and Baby Groot. At Halloween, Terri appears as a judge on the Food Network's *Outrageous Pumpkins* competition. As an international speaker, she loves speaking to young people about rising above adversity and fighting for their dreams.

www.terrihardin.com
www.youtube.com/terrihardinspeaks

Step Out of Your Comfort Zone and Tell Your Story

Melody Keymer Harper

As a speaking and a media coach, I train people how to speak so they stand out as a celebrity in their field, magnetically attract clients, and make more money. One of the most important things I teach is how to tell stories that connect with their audience.

I'm sure you've heard this many times, "Facts tell, stories sell." It's so true. People don't remember the facts, but they will remember a story that touches their emotions.

We all have many of our own stories to tell, but we don't realize what we've got. Some people are frightened to open up and talk about themselves, or they think it might be embarrassing or humiliating.

When you push yourself beyond your comfort zone, and beyond what you think you can do, your story reaches people. It connects with them. It makes them see you as more human and more relatable. There are people who need to hear what you have to share so they can realize they're not the only one who has gone through a similar situation or who has the same fear. Hearing your story will help them realize they're not alone. It will inspire them to go after what they want. The more painful it is for you to stand up in front of a group and tell your story, the more you're going to grow. I know this from experience.

My twin sister and I have been entertaining people since we were three years old. At 10, we went professional, and worked with some of the greatest film, TV, and stage performers: Elizabeth Taylor, Johnny Carson, Mickey Rooney, Jane Fonda, Betty White, Debbie Reynolds, and many more. We appeared in the movie *Double Trouble* with Elvis Presley and performed for USO shows all across the United States. During the years I've been performing, speaking, and teaching, I've shared plenty of interesting stories from that part of my life.

But only recently have I started telling this story, the one that has gone untold for decades because it's the most painful one for me to share. . .

All our lives, my twin and I were extremely close. We did everything together. We dressed alike. We performed together. She was my best friend, and I was hers. She wasn't Marilyn and I wasn't Melody—we were the Keymer twins. I loved being a twin.

As we grew into young adults, she began to feel like nobody knew her as herself. Everyone just knew her as a twin. Before our senior year in college, she eloped without telling me. I was shocked that she did something so momentous without me. It was hard for me to change my thinking so drastically and see us as separate individuals.

I struggled after her marriage. I dropped out of college. I took a huge risk and went on the road by myself. When I was approached to do a TV program, I thought, *This is great, but do I do it by myself?* We'd always been a duo. I didn't know who I was without my twin. I had to reinvent myself and figure out how to be okay doing it by myself.

She didn't understand how much it hurt that she was separating from me. And I didn't understand her need for her own identity. We didn't know how to communicate about it at the time. It was too painful. It pushed us apart.

After raising our kids, we came back together in business to develop an entrepreneurial program and to do our *Double Trouble*

Talk Radio Show. I loved doing our twin thing again. The intervening years gave us perspective and communication skills that allowed us to heal the hurt we both felt. I had come to recognize that my uniqueness was not just as a twin, but as an individual too. We're now complete together—and we're complete separately.

This story isn't like the light-hearted ones I've told for years about the people I've known and the experiences I've had as a performer. There are no celebrities in this story, and no funny punch lines. But it is a part of my life that touches deep emotions—first mine, and then my audience's. As difficult as it has been for me to finally tell this story, I know others will identify my story with their own struggles to create their identity separate from a parent, or a child, or a sibling, or a spouse, or a job—maybe even from a twin.

People love stories. How you tell them makes a huge difference. Get out of your comfort zone. Be authentic. Tell those tough stories you've got bottled up inside you. Grab people's hearts. The more emotion you can include in your story, the better it will connect with your audience. When you make them laugh or make them cry, you're golden.

※ ※ ※

Melody Keymer Harper, founder of Ignite Your Speaking Power, is an award-winning international speaker, communication expert, and seven-time bestselling author. She has over 40 years' experience in showbiz, and in the world of business, teaching, and speaking. She specializes in communication, storytelling, and stage-presence strategies. Aside from acting in the movie *Double Trouble* with Elvis Presley, Melody has worked with and shared the stage and screen with some of the most highly respected speaking giants including Brian Tracy, Les Brown, and Jack Canfield, and celebrities including Elizabeth Taylor, Johnny Carson, Suzanne Sommers, and Anthony Hopkins. She hosts her TV show and podcast, *Ignite Your Influence Now!* Her workshops and retreats are sought after by business professionals, speakers, authors, and entrepreneurs who want to get more high-paying clients, more speaking gigs, and more profits in their business.

www.igniteyourspeakingpower.com

Think of Challenges as Adventures

Jeni Herbst

I've been figuring out how to solve problems for most of my forty-plus years. Sometimes I've been more successful than others.

When my son, Kelvin, was born shortly after I turned 17, I did not give in to the pressure from my family to give him up. I knew I could figure out how to take care of us both. I made a promise to myself, and to my son, that I would do whatever it took to provide for him. When I made that promise, I didn't know what I was getting myself into. I was a young, single mother, on my own financially. But I figured it out. I kept that promise.

I've had plenty of opportunities to test my problem-solving skills, especially when it comes to Kelvin.

In order to advance my real estate career, I moved to Arizona when he was 19. He stayed in Wisconsin. It seemed like such a long distance, but I assured myself he was only a phone call away. So, a couple of years later when he stopped answering my phone calls for a month, I couldn't stop worrying. If you're a parent, you understand how hard that was for me. All he had to do was text or call and say, "Yes, Mom, I'm good," or "Yes, Mom, I'm busy." Anything would have been fine with me.

His girlfriend did answer my calls and said he was okay, but my instinct as a mother told me there was something wrong. I had to do something about it. That's the nurturing part of being a mother—you have to be there for your child, even when they're adults, and even when they don't return your calls.

I decided to fly to Wisconsin and surprise him. He **was** surprised to see me. Maybe my showing up unexpectedly taught him to not leave me hanging for so long. But he did not open up or tell me what was wrong. I could still sense something bothering him.

As we were saying goodbye at the airport, he was finally ready to talk. "Mom, there **is** something I want to tell you." He started to cry. "My landlord came to me about buying the duplex I live in. I have good credit, but I don't know if I want to become a landlord. I know nothing about real estate, but **you** do. So should I buy it?" He was in panic mode, excited yet fearful about the decision.

I was relieved it wasn't a bigger problem. And I wondered, *Is he finally willing to take my advice?*

I started asking him questions: How much is your landlord willing to sell the duplex for? What is it worth? What repairs does it need? Is the other tenant solid? Does he take care of his unit and pay the rent? Why does your landlord believe you should buy the property? We looked at what his responsibilities would be as a landlord.

Together we examined the positives and the negatives of this prospect. He decided to go for this amazing opportunity.

Because of my years as a loan originator and real estate investor, I was able to connect him with professionals who could get the deal done. I walked him through the process, and he was able to close in 30 days. At 21, he had his first investment property!

When the transaction was done, Kelvin said, "Mom, you may think that you're talking to the wall, but I still listen to you." It took me a moment to let that sink in.

I taught him what I do when fear starts to creep into my consciousness—I think of it as an adventure. I weigh the positives against the negatives. If I get past the negatives to all the positives and still feel excited, I go for it.

This experience with my son made two things clear to me. First, is the importance of trusting my instinct, especially as a mother. I knew there was something bothering him, and I didn't stop until we talked it out. Second, is the power we have as parents to inspire our children, to help them see opportunities they can't yet see for themselves, and to guide them to improve their lives and their financial situation.

Parents are role models for their children whether they realize it or not. It's gratifying when your children see how you live your life and follow in your footsteps.

Jeni Herbst, CEO of Prop1 Investments in Phoenix, is a full-time real estate investor and coach, with an extensive background in corporate banking, lending, and commercial management. Numerous facets of her real estate career include transaction specialist, pre-foreclosure expert, wholesaler, flipper, and property manager. She shares her knowledge through the Meetup group for women investors which she hosts. Her passion is serving teenagers, college students, low-income parents, and single parents by educating them about finance, real estate, and business so they can live the life they truly want to live. She is the proud mother of two adult children.

www.realestateandcoaching.com
www.meetup.com/AZ-Real-Estate-Estate-Inventing-Divas

To Diane &
Tom

Hope you Book
enjoy this
It is worth the
Read

Love you
Both

Joan

It's Never Too Late to Live with the Wind in Your Hair

Joan Howard

Being alive is one of the greatest gifts that we have. In my 85 years, I've had some rough spots, and I've had some great spots. But today is the best time of my life. I love everything about it. There's nothing else could I possibly want.

After eight decades of *pushing the limits*, here are a few of the things I do that make my life the gift it is.

Feel good about your appearance.

Every morning I get up and I get dressed. I do my hair. I put my jewelry on. I put my hearing aids on. Whether I stay in the house all day or go out, it doesn't make any difference. When I go up to the mailbox, I'm dressed. It's important to feel good about yourself. When you feel good, you'll do better.

Reward yourself.

After every big sale I ever made when I was in business, I bought myself something special. Sometimes it was a little tiny thing. Sometimes it was something big. Most of the art in my house came from me rewarding myself after I'd sold something big or did something well. Doing something to reward yourself helps you acknowledge your accomplishments and keeps you motivated to keep going.

Celebrate every chance you get, any way you can.

Nelson and I have been together for eight years. On our anniversary in 2020 during COVID, we decided to go up to Fountain Hills and watch the famous fountain. Since the pandemic hit, we had only cooked at home, so we decided to celebrate by buying food at a place by the fountain. As we ate our sandwiches in the park, we talked and watched the beautiful fountain shooting several hundred feet in the air. We watched the people running and walking with their dogs. It was a very pleasant day, and we made it special. It was our way of celebrating in the time of social distancing. Instead of saying, "Oh, poor us, we can't go to a fancy restaurant," we created an even more meaningful experience though simple celebration. Celebrate in ways that make you feel good, even if they're simple ways.

Don't let anything stop you.

Nelson and I love to ride his Harley. We met online when we were in our late 70s. Yes, even 70-somethings can find happiness online. Nelson's profile said, "I have a motorcycle and an extra helmet." I wrote back, "I'll take the helmet."

It only took half an hour on the back of his motorcycle for me to be sold. We couldn't hear each above the noise of the bike, but Nelson told me there were intercoms for motorcycles. I said, "Let's go buy one right now." I ended up replacing my tennis shoes with motorcycle boots, and I got a brand-new helmet. We outfitted ourselves with leather jackets and were ready to ride.

We used to spend every single, solitary weekend out on the bike. We rode over 75,000 miles—to Sturgis, Mount Rushmore, Colorado, California, and all over the state of Arizona. I loved the freedom on the bike.

When I started riding with Nelson, it never crossed my mind that it was dangerous. Never. I just got on the back, and that was the end of that.

My brothers thought we must be nuts. Nelson's kids did not think we were safe. "You guys are tooling around on the bike at

your age?" If my mother were alive, she would have just about killed me. But we had a great time, and we've got the pictures to prove it. It was the highlight of my life.

When we finally sold the bike, we bought a Jeep to take out every weekend. We still need to drive around with the wind in our hair.

Having Nelson in my life has added a unique atmosphere— everything is so different. Meeting him late in life, years after my husband died, made me realize that there is something else in life besides me or nothing. He is my best friend. In the summer of 2021, at 85 years old, Nelson and I got married. We felt a Hawaiian wind in our hair on our honeymoon. Finding each other and enjoying our life together in our 80s proves that it's never too late to embrace those gifts life keeps giving you.

※ ※ ※

Joan Howard is a retired business consultant and entrepreneur. After being fired from every job she ever had, she started her own company as a telecommunications systems contractor. In the 1980s, it was rare to see any female-owned contractors in Arizona. Many men told her they didn't expect her to succeed, but she was able to thrive and prove them all wrong. She has owned a variety of businesses and continues to manage her real estate investments. For over 35 years, Joan has held leadership positions at Impact for Enterprising Women, a networking group for female professionals and business owners. She is a fierce advocate for women, and has taken the group to a higher level, providing scholarships and educational opportunities for women.

www.joanhoward@cox.net
www.impactforenterprisingwomen.org

Competition Builds Confidence

Linda Howell

The confidence you gain as an athlete, striving for excellence every day, helps you get through difficult times and successfully deal with stress in every area of your life.

My whole childhood involved performing and competing. As a youngster, I played flute and tried out for orchestras and bands. I competed against other flutists for first chair. When I got up in front of my entire junior high assembly and played "Ave Maria," I was exhilarated. I didn't let the fear of competing stop me from going for it.

I started playing tennis when I was eight years old. I made it to the finals in my first tournament, then lost to a girl who was taller than me. But that was okay. You have to lose in order to learn to get better.

This whole idea that competition is bad has a lot to do with how individual parents deal with competition, and what they pass along to their children.

Any kind of competition presented in a positive way, without improper expectations from coaches or parents, is absolutely vital to growing up in this very competitive and stressful world. It's important to learn at a young age that it's okay to put yourself out there—and that you're going to lose. You're definitely going to lose. You make yourself better when you compete against yourself and others. We take away from children's growth when we don't let them experience losing. How do they learn to be better next time if they always win?

You also learn to seek out guidance, education, and information to perform better the next time. I never stop learning, even for a minute. I will admit my failures and strive to learn from somebody else.

Growing up, my parents instilled in me the belief that I had to succeed. They didn't care if it was my grades or sports or music—they taught me that if I worked hard, I would succeed. They never pushed me to go one direction or another. They never questioned whether I was going to make enough money or have enough prestige. And they never pressured me to win. They supported me in following wherever my passion led.

The only thing my parents insisted on—other than me working hard—was, "Don't throw your tennis racket. Be a good sport. Be a good person. As long as you love the sport, continue on."

What competition instilled in me at a young age was respect, integrity, and the ability to perform in stressful situations.

I have taken that attitude of striving for excellence right into my life and my career. I tackle everything I do that same way. *I do not fail. I will not fail.* I'm not one to sit back and let fear stop me from taking on a challenge.

I attribute my ability to perform under stress to playing professional sports. When you play sports at a high level, your body learns to deal with stress in a different way. My training and time in competitive sports where I had to perform in stressful moments have helped me succeed in life.

When I took my Playing Ability Test to become a PGA member, my hands were shaking to the nth degree. I had to make the last putt to pass the test. Talk about pressure! My training kicked in, and I passed on my first try.

In my 20s, when I was teaching tennis at Riviera Country Club in Los Angeles, I had to speak in front of a large group of members. My heart was pounding to the point I thought I was going to pass out. When I finished and stepped down, somebody said, "Wow, Linda, that was wonderful. What a great job." *Say what?* I remember standing up in front of the group, but I have no idea what I said. My body just did what I had trained it to do.

Being six foot tall, people think I'm confident and know what I'm doing the minute I walk in a room. But that's not always the case. It's funny, but I believe my lack of complete confidence in every situation is a positive trait. It motivates me to gain more confidence by asking for help and continuing to learn. If I get to the point where I think I've got it all figured out, that's where I'm going to have problems. Maybe that's why I'm so strange—I'm not completely confident, yet I am.

I am not always fearless, but I do new things regardless. I look back at so many times in my life and think, *Boy, that took some courage.* After injuries ended my tennis career, it took guts when I started an alternative fitness business. When I sold that business at 38, I started at the bottom with golf. I worked at a municipal golf course for $7.50 an hour and free golf. Free golf was a big motivator! Now I'm a PGA Class "A" pro, running a successful golf course, getting accolades from the USGA and the PGA.

When opportunities presented themselves, I took a step that was a little out of my comfort zone—or **a lot** out of my comfort zone. I trusted my ability to deal with stress because of my athletic training. I took opportunities that were available and moved ahead without questioning them. If I hadn't had those competitive experiences, I can't imagine that I would be where I am today.

Build your confidence by putting yourself in situations where you are "on stage" and have to perform. It doesn't have to be sports. It doesn't have to be a big stage. Just put yourself out there in front of people and perform. Trust your instincts and allow yourself to take advantage of the unique opportunities that will come your way.

Competing will build your confidence and ability to handle stressful situations. When you have the courage to take that first step, and the passion to continue forward, you'll be successful.

❋ ❋ ❋

Linda Howell is the PGA Director of Golf for Towa Golf Course at Buffalo Thunder Resort and Casino in Santa Fe, New Mexico. She has won multiple awards personally as well as for properties she headed and was inducted into the San Diego State University Hall of Fame in 2020. She is a PGA Class "A" member and has had great success instructing players ranging from beginners to experts. Before she turned her career focus to golf, Linda played professional tennis, ranking in the top 100, competing at Wimbledon, the U.S. Open, and the Australian Open. She has increased female participation in sports through women's specialty clinics and The First Tee life skills program for teens. She won the PGA Youth Development Award in 2018. Linda is an admitted overachiever whose mission is to show that more women can become successful in a man's world.

www.hiltonbuffalothunder.com/golf
Wikipedia: Linda Howell

Love the Person Who's Looking Back at You in the Mirror

Laura Jaramillo

In a past relationship, my partner shocked me when they said, "I feel like I love you more than you love yourself."

That made me stand back and wonder, *What does loving myself mean? What does it even look like?* I had been wired to give and give and give, then have nothing left for myself. I asked myself, *What are some things I do when I'm in love with someone?* One is I text them: "I love you." So, I started texting myself "I love you." I wouldn't check my phone until I felt a need to send love to myself. But I started to think about who I am.

I've always been positive and active. I always want to see the good in people. I love to move around. I love to dance. I love going to events where I can DJ and entertain people. Before COVID, I was always on the go. I was DJing night after night. I was traveling a lot.

A few months before COVID, I injured my foot and wasn't able to walk without crutches. That injury slowed me down but didn't stop me. Then COVID hit, and the world went silent. There was no place to go. No place to escape to. I was alone with my own thoughts. They kept asking: *Okay, who are you, really? Do you love yourself?*

People were wearing masks because of the virus. But I was

wearing a mask under my mask. I was hiding. My heart was feeling so heavy and so hard. For three months I was in my room, alone, crying, and crying, and crying. *Who am I? Maybe the person that I've been embodying hasn't truly been 100% who I am.*

I discovered this trauma within myself that I didn't even realize was there. I didn't feel safe being who I am. So, I started to delve into questions of self-identity.

Before I was forced to slow down and look inside, I went to my event spaces to DJ from eight o'clock at night till two o'clock in the morning. At these events, in these places, I could express who I was because I felt safe. But when I was in other spaces—a business meeting or with my parents—I crawled back inside the shell of a persona I thought people wanted me to be. I showed up how I thought I **had** to show up. No wonder I didn't know how to love myself. I didn't know who I was.

This pandemic gave me the chance to really sit and say, *No, the person that people thought I was, that's not who I am. This is who I truly am.* This introspection allowed me to embrace my identity as nonbinary.

Out of that quiet time of reflection came this understanding of the duality of my identity. I had to go inside and heal in order to find the balance of the divine feminine and the divine masculine energies within me. Identifying now as non-binary feels authentic—and liberating.

There was this instant where I knew I could translate my inner transformation into my external world. I have embodied my real identity—minus any of my parents' expectations—not just with my closest friends and my family, but in every single space and place that I go.

I fully express myself—sometimes more masculine, sometimes more feminine. I no longer think there is only a certain way that I have to show up. Now I can live freely.

Along with my transformation, I realized that trauma lies

deep within the LGBTQ+ community. When the tragic Pulse nightclub shooting occurred a few years ago, our community was hurt emotionally, if not physically. We're still hurting. There are only a few nightclubs here in Orlando where we feel safe, and gender non-conforming individuals lack safe **daytime** places where they can express their identity. That led me to form a nonprofit that is creating imaginative spaces with coffee shops, personal services, and medical services that provide safe places for the LGBTQ+ community to gather.

It brings my heart so much joy to feel confident in sharing who I am, and helping others feel free to do the same. I can embody both the feminine and the masculine. I can put on a dress today and cut all my hair off tomorrow. I can be an ever-changing canvas, choosing whatever I want to express.

This liberation allows me to feel safe enough to open up and love the person who is looking back at me in the mirror and write songs that are lullabies to myself.

❋ ❋ ❋

Laura Jaramillo, known professionally as **Lauralite,** was born in Cali, Colombia. They are an entrepreneur, immersive event and media production professional, Airbnb management specialist, and consciousness mentor. At age four, they moved to the United States with their family, hoping to escape the violence and turmoil that permeated the area, and seeking political asylum as a refugee. They wrote their first song at eight years old and haven't given up on the dream since. Their upcoming, seven-song debut E.P, *Everything That's Wrong with Me,* highlights the journey of learning to truly and unconditionally love oneself. Determined to promote self-positivity, their free-spirited personality and radiant vocals help to soothe the soul and encourage self-healing, all the while reminding listeners that, "It's OK to not be OK, but it's not OK to stay that way." In 2020, they co-founded the Please Evolve Foundation and started the Please Bloom Initiative branch, an organization navigating the future of LGBTQ+ progress by building spaces curated for the community's empowerment and success.

www.pleasebloom.org
Facebook.com/LauraLiteMusic

You're a Woman—Embrace It

Isabel Kozak

For me, I find it wonderful to be a woman. I would not want to be a man. For how I am—how driven I am, how outspoken I am—I am thankful I'm a woman.

I believe women look at things differently. We bring family into it. We bring personality into it. We may even bring our faith into it. We are dynamic and a great force.

But why are women CEOs so few and far between? How do we set limits on ourselves?

For women to be competitive in this world and have a place in the boardroom, we have to be educated. Education helps us push limits, get to that glass ceiling, and reach the top of agencies and companies.

If you don't take steps toward getting an education, you can't complain, "It's always a man in charge." Or "Why is it that women aren't in charge?" Let's take care of that. Go back to school, find your passion, and figure out what you want to do.

If you want to do accounting, be the best accountant you can be. If you want to be in management, be the best manager you can be. Set your goals and do it.

I pushed so many limits to get where I am today. I didn't say to myself, *Oh, woe is me. It was such a hard adjustment when I moved all the way from the Philippines to the U.S.* No! Put away all the excuses. If you want to do something, do it. I traveled from the other end of the earth to a strange place with nobody I knew except my husband. It didn't stop me. Nothing should stop you.

My calling has always been to be somebody who can help. That's why first teaching and then medicine were careers I chose.

Nursing was something that spoke to me because I really liked that caring and compassion part of the job. After working as head nurse in an emergency room for a year, I started noticing what was happening to older folks who were brought in. The doctors told us, "Oh, just put them in the back corner. They probably have a urinary tract infection." I couldn't ignore them. I'd go talk to them and their families and find out how I could help.

I said to myself, *I can do it better than those male ER doctors.* So, I went back to school for my fourth degree, and became a nurse practitioner in a geriatrics program—until I decided to take on a new challenge and try something else.

When I was offered the job in orthopedics at the Phoenix Veterans Administration hospital, I knew nothing about orthopedics. But they offered to train me. I wanted to move to Phoenix, the VA was going to pay for the move, and it was something I had not done. Why not take on the challenge?

I was the first woman in that male-dominated department. Along with my skills, I brought my woman's viewpoint. I looked at things from the perspective of a nurse, from the perspective of a patient, and from the perspective of a woman. Within six months, I was the head of the department.

I love orthopedics and have assisted in surgery for almost 20 years. It is a challenge, but more importantly, it's helping another person. That's what motivates me. Not the money. Not the title. It's when the veteran who had spine surgery said to me, "Oh my God, Dr. Kozak, you saved my life. If you hadn't done the surgery, I'd be in a wheelchair." He's very thankful. He's a productive member of society. He's happy with his wife and can take care of his kids. I do it for people like him.

I ran the orthopedics department until I got my fifth degree—a doctorate in nursing leadership administration. In my position as assistant chief of staff, I continue to push the limits and tackle more projects that require a global perspective to solutions.

Where I am now is physician-dominated, but I'm able to push that boundary. Why? Because I am educated.

I've done all these things, but there's so much more to do. There's so much more to explore. There's so much more to build. There are so many more people to help. It's never about what we have already done. There's so much more we women can do.

Sit down and think, *What do I really want to do for myself?* If you're uncomfortable with something, that's even better. Challenge yourself. Then educate yourself. You can be very successful in whatever you want to do.

We make ourselves what we are. We're never done. It's not about what you have done. It's about what you will do next.

Women look at the world in a different way. Let's not lose that. Cherish your ability to see things differently and do things differently.

Welcome new challenges. Be open to opportunities. Be positive. Claim your power.

You're a woman—embrace it.

❋ ❋ ❋

Dr. Isabel Kozak is the Assistant Chief of Staff for Community Medicine at the Phoenix Veterans Administration Health Care System. She was born and raised in the Philippines where she obtained two bachelor's degrees and was a teacher. After settling permanently in the United States at 23, she followed her lifelong dream and pursued a nursing degree and a career in medicine. Isabel left her work as the head emergency room nurse in an ICU to earn a master's degree in nursing, her fourth degree. After becoming a certified adult nurse practitioner, she moved into the male-centric field of orthopedics and orthopedic surgeries. She joined the VA as a nurse practitioner in orthopedics and was quickly named head of the department. She graduated summa cum laude in 2015 with her fifth degree, a doctorate in nursing leadership administration. In 2017, she co-founded the Veggies for Veterans program to address food insecurity of homeless and low-income veterans. In addition to her busy work schedule, Isabel makes time for her husband, two sons, her dog, an archery hobby, and charity work. When something is important to her, she finds time for it.

Email: IKozak@cox.net

Never Ever Quit

Anne Lorimor

During my nine decades on Earth, life has given me plenty of opportunities—and some good reasons—to quit. Though my life hasn't always been easy, I never quit.

Life was difficult growing up during the Great Depression, the oldest of 10 children. We were miserably poor—sometimes cold or hungry. For a short time, we lived out of a homemade trailer and a truck with a canvas top. Another time we lived in a tent with no floor, no electricity, no telephone, and no running water. We were homeless, but never hopeless.

I have always loved to learn. When I was 15, I read that you had to be super intelligent to go to college. I told my teacher, "Well, I guess that washes me out." She reassured me that I'd have no trouble in college, and encouraged me to keep working toward that goal, to never quit. At first I wasn't able to finish college, so I got my nursing degree to fall back on. When I finished nursing school, I spent the money I'd been saving for college and bought a cow for my mother. She and my younger siblings were living in primitive conditions and needed the cow to help feed themselves. Then I had to figure out how to earn enough money to get back to college.

In spite of many setbacks, I kept going. With the help of wonderful teachers, mentors, benefactors, scholarships, part-time jobs, and hard work, I found ways to support myself and stay in school. Altogether, I've earned a registered nursing degree, two bachelor's degrees, two master's degrees, and a Ph.D.

I never quit.

Thirty years ago, when my doctor told me I had lymphoma and had a 50/50 chance of being alive in a year, I knew I had not done what I needed to do to take care of myself. In addition to the chemo, I did biofeedback, meditation, and guided imagery. I did everything I could think of to reduce my stress and get in shape. I'm still healthy today. I call myself a victor, not a survivor.

When I decided to climb Mt. Kilimanjaro and set the Guinness World Record, I thought that would be a dramatic way to get more attention and more money for the kids my foundation supports. It was a wonderful way to combine my two passions—my lifelong love of hiking and helping underserved kids.

When I was 85, I set the record as the oldest woman to summit Mt. Kilimanjaro. Four months later, an older woman claimed that record. So, I decided to do it again, and to do it better. I believe that nothing is ever hopeless, no matter how impossible my situation seemed. It is really important to me that I not give up.

I started training like mad. My goal was to set the record as **the oldest person** to reach that summit. I trained even harder than before, doing everything I could to get very, very fit. I wanted to be in the best shape possible, so I trained hard and trained carefully. I hiked every day. I was careful not to climb on paths if there was any chance of slipping or falling.

On our way to Kilimanjaro, we spent time on a safari gradually getting used to the higher elevations. The only day it rained on us, I stepped on a rubber mat on wooden steps, and it slipped right out from under me. Down I went. I hurt, but I still kept on going.

Two days before we were due to summit, I was really, really hurting. But I could not quit. A lot of people were counting on me, and a film crew was there to do a documentary. I said, "Nobody wants a documentary of a failed climb. I've got to do this."

So, we said prayers and pushed on. I kept sitting down a lot more than I had the time before, but that was not surprising. I was in great pain, but I did not know I had broken three ribs until I visited my doctor after I returned home.

In 2019, I set the Guinness World Record as the oldest **person** to summit Mt. Kilimanjaro. It was exciting to see the curvature of the earth from 19,341 feet high. What a thrill to see the stars down around our ears as we hiked. They were so brilliant. And I was terribly excited to see the Southern Cross, which we don't see in the Northern Hemisphere.

I haven't had an easy life, but I never let myself get stopped. Sometimes now I let myself get slowed down. But even when I'm taking those breaks, I'm not stopping, I'm doing something to move me toward my next goal. In 2022, I'm going to Machu Picchu to hike for my 92nd birthday and raise more money for the kids.

I think a lot of what keeps me going is simply making up my mind to do something. At 91 years old, I have a focus that fulfills me—the kids my foundation helps. Creating Exciting Futures is showing underprivileged children and youth their options and giving them the tools to reach their full potential, lead lives they love, and pay it forward.

On the days when I'd just like to stay in bed, I tell myself, "No, no, no. Let's just keep going. There are important things out there to be done that'll help other people and the world."

Here are the principles that guide my life.

- **Keep yourself fit and healthy.** No matter what you do in life, if you feel good, it's easier to do.
- **Get deeply involved with a cause greater than yourself.** Find opportunities to volunteer so you can use your time productively and meaningfully. You'll feel good about yourself.

You'll give back to others. And you'll meet people that you find interesting and exciting.

- **Never, ever give up.** Don't let people discourage you. Find a way to do what is important to you. You decide what you can do, and then do it.

Let these principles guide your life too.

❋ ❋ ❋

Anne Lorimor holds the Guinness World Record as the oldest person to reach the summit of Mt. Kilimanjaro when she was 89 years old. She has traveled in more than 100 countries and lived for extended periods of time in Egypt and Nigeria. Recognizing that our future is our youth, she founded Lorimor Child Empowerment Foundation DBA Creating Exciting Futures. Having experienced severe poverty as a child, Anne continues working to help kids from low-income families realize they have options other than living the rest of their lives in poverty. She continues to train daily for her upcoming trip to Machu Picchu, a trip that will raise awareness and money for her foundation.

www.creatingexcitingfutures.org

Know What Your Heart Wants

Carrie Lu

After getting my MBA at Rutgers, I was hired by Citibank as a management associate. There were 16 of us in a program that put us on the fast track to management positions. As I participated in the group calls week after week, it didn't take long to realize I was the only one who was working 10 to 12 hours a day. Everyone else seemed to have easy jobs working nine to five. I was thinking to myself, *How come I'm the only one who has to work so hard?* But deep down, I felt, *There must be a reason why I'm doing this.*

When Citibank moved me to Las Vegas and assigned me to manage a team of 80 people, I realized all my hard work had built the foundation for operating at a higher, more difficult level. But taking on this new position with so many people to manage scared me. I was only in my late 20s. I had four experienced managers reporting to me who were in their 40s and who had worked for Citibank for 10 to 20 years. I decided my goal was to take care of my people and to do whatever needed to be done to ensure the success of the team. There wasn't one thing I wouldn't do—from getting coffee to fixing the copier. Yes, I was their manager, and they were my employees, but they were not my servants.

Gradually, I realized that corporate America was not the place for me. I didn't feel like I was making a difference. My opinions were not valued—or even heard. I did not see that I was able to provide a lot of value other than speaking up for my employees who were working hard.

I found that often managers cared more about themselves than they did about their people. Many focused on only making sure they got a great annual review so they could get a salary increase or a bonus. It was such a disempowering experience.

I needed to make a change. I was willing to give up a job with great pay and four weeks of vacation. It was a lot more important for me to be happy. Following my heart and my instinct is what would be good for my soul.

When I started my career in the Las Vegas residential real estate world in 2007, not one person supported me. Not one person said, "Oh, good for you. If you're unhappy at Citibank, then I'm glad you're pursuing something you want." Everyone said, "Are you **crazy**? You have an MBA degree and you're going to become a Realtor®?" It didn't matter to me if other people agreed with me or not. They were not living my life.

A year later, the real estate market crashed. It would have been very easy for me to say, *Well, this is going to be really hard. I'll just give up. I'll look for a full-time position, go back to a corporate job, and be done with it.* But I did not want to work for people who did not share the same values and goals I did. My heart was not in it to work for somebody else anymore.

So, I followed my heart. I stayed in real estate and learned as much as I could about how to do well in this business. In my second year, I closed 20 transactions and my income surpassed what I was making at Citibank.

Fourteen years later, people are surprised that I'm still in real estate. Even my parents want me to get a full-time job in the corporate world. That's not going to happen. I love what I'm doing. Real estate has taken me on a journey of self-discovery. I learn more about myself with every transaction.

I enjoy helping people find the American dream of homeownership. It's a great feeling to have a stable career in the business of my own choice. Nobody can take that away from me. If I had still been working for Citibank, I could have been laid off and had to look for another job.

As we're dealing with the challenges of COVID, I've worked on building my relationships with my current clients, past clients, and future clients. I am not just focused on selling real estate, but on being sensitive to the needs of other human beings who are going through tough times. Because so many people have financial troubles, I ask if there is anything I can help them with—like connecting them to a wonderful homeowner insurance agent or auto insurance agent who can help reduce their monthly expenses. That's what I've been focusing on.

Give it your best, no matter what happens. Always provide value. Treat people fairly. And most of all, never give up on what your heart wants.

✳ ✳ ✳

Carrie (Xiao-Qing) Lu, is a residential Realtor® with Signature Real Estate Group SW in Las Vegas. Prior to entering real estate in 2007, she spent eight years in corporate America in a variety of roles: engineering consultant, financial consultant for companies including AT&T and Deutsche Bank, financial manager at Prudential Financial, and vice president at Citibank. Carrie has a bachelor's degree and MBA from Rutgers. During her off-time, she is active in local animal rescue organizations. She loves cats and has fostered over 100 abandoned and homeless kittens and adult cats.

Email:carrie@LasVegasRealtyTeam.com

Maintaining Faith and Hope

Yvette McDowell

I've experienced so many things that would cause other people to lose their faith and their hope. I've dealt with life and death. I've had more blood on my hands—literally—than you can imagine. But that's part of life. We all go through challenges, some worse than others. We can either deal with it in a manner that moves us forward, or we can shut down. I choose to keep moving forward.

As an African American woman, I grew up in a setting where racism and sexism were rampant and commonplace. All the racial epithets were part and parcel of my growing up. That's history.

As I was going through the Pasadena Fire Department Training Academy in the early 80s, I heard many stories from African American male firefighters about the challenges they went through just because they were men of color. What did that mean for me? *I'm a female of color, so I've got a couple of strikes against me already.*

Some of the guys did not want females in the department, period. There was a machismo attitude that women need to have babies, stay in the kitchen, and be seen but not heard. One captain rode me harder than he rode the men. He had me take a heavy wooden ladder off the fire engine, throw it up against the wall, and extend it—over and over and over. My shoulders hurt like you wouldn't believe, but I kept at it. The men may have more body strength, but I wasn't a weakling. I was determined to get through the training and didn't even give myself an option to quit. I never said, "I can't." That's a word that just doesn't exist for me.

When I was a newbie in the department, another captain said straight out, "We've never had a Black female survive on this department." I looked right back at him and said, "You've got your first one now." I set out to master my job, and I proved I could do it. My motto was: *Let your performance speak, not your mouth.*

From my experience as a paramedic and firefighter, I know there is nothing more revealing or stressful than dealing with death and dying. A mistake can be very costly. I've seen life every which way you can imagine it. Suicides, murders, accidents—you name it, I've treated it all. There were times when I was kneeling in front of someone, assessing them, and all of a sudden, they stopped breathing. That's real life.

In 1993, while I was with the fire department, I was also going to law school part time and clerking for the city prosecutor. When tragedy struck Pasadena, I was unexpectedly drawn into the world of gangs. In what became known as the Halloween Massacre, three teens who were on their way home from trick-or-treating were mistaken for gang members by a rival gang. The gang members fired on them, killing all three teens and wounding several others.

My partner and I were in the first responding paramedic unit that was called out. Running that scene was unreal—bodies lying around, mothers weeping over their kids. One of the victims was the son of my dear friend. That made it that even more intense.

In the aftermath, the city prosecutor started searching for programs we could put together to address this gang issue. Our team created the Community Partnership Against Gangs program, and I was hired to be the coordinator.

I loved working with gang members and families. It taught me about the dynamics behind that culture. When I got down deep with these folks, I found some very vulnerable individuals. Believe me, a lot of these gang members have hearts. They have feelings. Often, it's a family dynamic that leads a young person to join a gang. Some are straight out hardcore and don't want to stop doing what they're doing. But a lot of kids don't know what they're getting into. They want to do things better, and don't know how to. With the resources and education we provided, our program made a positive impact in the community.

One day on my way home, I heard Stevie Wonder's new song *Conversation Peace* on the radio. I was so moved by the lyrics that I wanted to create a project around that theme. When I shared my idea for a film with the city prosecutor, she wanted us to run with it. We created the concept, and the local cable access channel produced a documentary called *Conversation Peace*. (We did get permission to use this song from Stevie Wonder's folks.)

The film started off with footage of the horrible scenes from the Halloween Massacre, then moved forward to a discussion around peace and what we can do to stem the tide of gang violence. In the film I appeared with gang members walking into court and walking onto a construction job site.

Never in my wildest dreams could I have imagined strolling down the red carpet and walking on stage when *Conversation Peace* won an Emmy Award. It was totally unreal. We will never repair the devastation done to people of color by the war on drugs, but I was proud of what we **were** accomplishing, and thrilled that we received such public recognition for our work.

I've learned to always put humankind first. Whenever I see wrong being done, no matter who the person is, or what color they are, I'm ready to fight for justice. I believe wholeheartedly we are put here to uplift people. We are to use our time on this earth to make it a better place for the next person. My faith requires me to pull people up, not push people down.

Success to me is not about plaques or commendations or how much money I make. No. Success is truly seeing people come into who they are and then being able to pay it forward. When someone tells me, "My life changed because of what you said," **that's** success. That keeps me going.

I've never lost faith. I've never lost hope. I've never lost optimism. There's still more for me to do. I have no idea what's next, but I have a Lord above who does know. When he prompts me to move, that's what I'll be doing.

❋ ❋ ❋

Yvette McDowell has excelled in various careers as a firefighter/paramedic, city prosecutor, trial attorney, and cannabis law consultant. She strives to educate leaders about the cannabis industry and works with government agencies on proposed regulations directly relating to the industry and on the creation and correct implementation of social equity plans. Yvette is currently serving a second two-year term on the California Cannabis Industry Association's Board of Directors, and co-chairs the Diversity, Inclusion, and Social Equity Committee. Under her leadership, this committee produced a well-received document which seeks to provide alternative language to common terms used in the cannabis industry that are racially divisive. She participates in numerous professional organizations including the International Cannabis Bar Association as co-chair, Minority Cannabis Business Association, Los Angeles County Bar Association's Cannabis Section, Orange County Women Leaders in Law Enforcement as co-chair, and is a Southern California speaker for Law Enforcement Action Partnership (LEAP).

www.yvettemcdowell.com

Put *Your* Oxygen Mask on First

Monica McKenna

When my last relationship came to an abrupt end, I was left with almost nothing—my clothes, my car, and a couple hundred dollars in my bank account. I was scared.

I'd been single, in and out of relationships, for nine years, living paycheck to paycheck, and relying on men to support me. My job as a flight attendant gave me opportunities to meet a lot of wealthy men. When I was in a relationship with one, life was amazing. But as soon as the next younger, cuter version of me came along, I was pushed to the side. Then I would start over—again.

It was a pattern I kept repeating. I was searching for the right person who I thought would take care of me. I was attracting the wrong people, the wrong men. I wasn't standing on my own two feet, and I wasn't feeling very good about myself. I was desperate. I was miserable—and lost. Definitely lost.

With that last terrible breakup, I hit rock bottom. Driving away from his house and heading for LA, I had a huge realization—I needed to put on my own oxygen mask. I needed to not rely on anyone else. I needed to get my life together. It was my responsibility to change my life, to make it what I wanted to make it—for myself.

I started thinking about my grown children, about what kind of legacy I was going to leave for them. *What happens if they need me and I'm not even able to support myself?* I was really frightened. There had to be more than just going from relationship to relationship and relying on men. I knew I had to change. I had to create my own security so it could never be taken from me again—ever. **I** had to be the person I was looking for.

A lot of fears came up as I struggled to just take care of the basic necessities. *Where do I go? Where do I turn? How do I turn this around?*

It brings tears to my eyes remembering how that deep-rooted message came through loud and clear: *Stop the madness. That's enough of that. Enough!*

The pain was what I needed to shift my mindset. I realized that I **do** have the power to change my life, and that I had to do something NOW!

Embracing that desire gave me new purpose. I shifted from looking back in the rearview mirror to looking forward. So many questions spun around in my head: *What can I do? Where can I start? What abilities do I have? How can I get there? Who can help me?*

I realized there was one valuable asset I did have left. I had no money, but I did have really good credit. I chose to use that credit to invest in myself and my future by hiring a coach and joining a mastermind.

And then the right people started showing up.

My fabulous coach shined a light on a new path for me and brought me to a fresh level of awareness. I showed him a video that I had done years ago with the goal of starting up a nonprofit organization. He could see something I couldn't see. He looked at me and said, "I want to know where **that** girl's at." I thought about it. "You know what? **That** girl is deep inside me. She's going to come out again. She's going to be my focus."

Every day, that drive to become who I truly am, pushed me

forward.

I created an avatar for myself from a luggage tag I had with this blonde flight attendant on it. When I looked at that tag, I saw this character that looked so happy, so full of joy, so free. I was already a flight attendant—and blonde—but not a happy one. She became my avatar. It may sound strange, but identifying with her gave me a feeling of power. When I was flying, I'd look down at this tag and tell myself, *You've got this, girl. You've got this!*

When I stepped into my power and allowed myself to visualize and dream, things started happening. I took action every single day, even when I was scared to death. With the support of my coach and my cheerleaders in the group, I took little, baby actions. *Start dreaming. Start visualizing. Take one step, then another. What's next? Why aren't you doing this? You know how to do it, how come you're not doing it? Stop using money as an excuse.* I'm an expert at coming up with creative excuses not to do something. But my coach wouldn't let me get away with that.

Through the mastermind group, I connected with investors that enabled me to start buying Airbnb properties. I became a *Superhost.* I was on a roll. Stepping through my fear and taking daily consistent action, I kept moving forward.

Sometimes we'll do more for others than we'll do for ourselves. My coach brought me back to my roots of putting on my own oxygen mask.

It's never too late to change. You may be hiding your power, but you **do** have it within you. Put on your own oxygen mask.

Believe that you can do it. Know that you are enough. Ask for help. Pull your strength from within. Take small actions daily toward your goal.

So—dream it, believe it, and live it. It's possible. You've got this, girl!

✳ ✳ ✳

Monica McKenna founded Pineapple Queen Coaching in 2020, making another of her dreams come true. She coaches hundreds of men and women to navigate their lives with accountability, synergy, strategy, and empowerment. Her online courses, webinars, and summits are viewed worldwide. She is a real estate investor and an Airbnb Superhost. Monica is a former flight attendant, a bestselling Amazon author, a podcast host, and has created and produced a national talk show. Her viral videos have made her an influencer on TikTok. She is grateful for being given a chance to make a difference in this crazy, big, beautiful world!

Podcast: *Thrive and Shine with Pineapple Queen & Miss Bright Ideas*
Facebook group: Self-Love Series 2021

Martial Arts Changed Me

Melodee Meyer

I became a single parent of two young boys after leaving a very abusive marriage, a relationship with a lot of domestic violence. My pain tolerance was even higher than my forgiveness level. Many times I feared for my life. I may look like the least likely person you would ever expect to be in a situation like that, but I spent time in the hospital and in a women's shelter.

Growing up, my very religious family taught me to believe in marriage, and that love could conquer anything. I stayed because I thought I could help my husband and that we could work it out. One day during a marriage counseling session, my pastor said, "I just have to say something. You're here for marriage counseling, but you're here by yourself. That's a problem." I thought I was being strong taking care of someone else—everyone else. He helped me realize I needed to start taking care of myself.

I learned not to use somebody else as an excuse for my current situation. This wasn't being done **to** me. Yes, I was hit. But I had co-created an environment where this was acceptable. I was victimized, but I was not a victim.

Because I was afraid that my ex-husband would do something terrible to us, I worked hard at protecting myself and my sons. When I saw it affecting my children, I knew that I had to make a choice. I had to choose a life for my sons that was without violence and without fear.

Why is it that we are willing to do something for someone else but not do what we need to do for ourselves? Imagine if you were to see your five-year-old daughter being attacked. You'd know exactly what to do in that moment. You'd do anything you could to protect her. You'd be absolutely clear about what it is you wanted.

But for many women, when it comes to ourselves, we can't protect ourselves to the same degree because we're not as clear about what we want. If we don't know what we want, we can't actually go after it.

After experiencing the abuse from the outside, I turned that abuse within and became abusive to myself with bulimia. Clearly, I needed to be proactive about my relationship with myself.

It's convenient to adopt that victim mentality and tell yourself, *I don't know what I want. Nothing is happening for me.* When you take responsibility for your situation, you actually have to do something about it. Not everyone wants that. For many years, as long as I was taking care of other people, I didn't take responsibility for myself.

I'm really grateful my kids helped me see I needed to leave the marriage. I don't know how much longer I would have, or could have, put up with the abuse. My concern for my sons' safety and emotional health moved me to take action and work to build a wonderful life with them that we never could have had if I'd stayed.

When martial arts came along, it was a positive next step in taking care of myself. It helped me build up my confidence and my skill set so I could take care of myself at a higher level.

Martial arts changed me. I never intended to get into it. I questioned why I was even looking at it at all. I'm not into fighting. I just really want to get along with everyone.

People think martial arts is all about fighting. But here's the key—it's really about **stopping** the fight, not starting the fight.

The truth is, the fight isn't going on outside of us; the fight is within. That's the fight we need to stop. We need to be more in cooperation with ourselves—with our higher self, with who we really are, with what our values are. That's where our power comes from, not from being against something and going into that fear place.

When I really got in touch with that in my own life, I knew martial arts was the direction to go. I started on this path over 20 years ago and now hold a 6th-degree black belt and the designation of "Master."

I was busy taking care of everybody else—two boys, my business, my clients, my students. Then one day I woke up and wondered, *What do I want?* That's a question that I never allowed myself to ask before. I had been taught that kind of thinking was selfish. *Who am I? What do I want? What is important to me? What's my purpose? Why am I here on this planet? What are my gifts?* These questions are so simple but so big, that I had shied away from them all together.

When I was clearer about what I wanted, I could protect myself and stand up for myself. No more letting other people roll over my boundaries or trample my values.

When I was clear, I could let go of those outdated beliefs that were keeping me small.

Everything on the outside is a manifestation of what's going on in the inside. When you want to change your life, change your belief system. When you want to change your business, change your belief system. When you want to transform your relationships, change your belief system. When you want to change your body, you can do that too. It's your belief system that put you in that particular body or business or relationship. When you want to change what's on the outside, change what's on the inside first.

❋ ❋ ❋

Melodee Meyer is an entrepreneur and coach who, for over three decades, has empowered mission-driven entrepreneurs to create a healthy business and a healthy body so they can fulfill their purpose and make a positive impact in the world. She has worked in the fitness, television, and travel sectors with companies such as Amazon, CBS's *Survivor*, MTV, The Outdoor Channel, Sprint, Amadeus, *Competitor Magazine*, eDiets, and Entrepreneurs TV Network. She has a master's degree in spiritual psychology, is a 6th degree Black Belt, and was inducted into the United States Martial Arts Hall of Fame in 2020. After overcoming many challenges in her life including bullying, domestic violence, and life as a single mom, she has gone on to build a seven-figure business. As a national speaker, Melodee uses the lessons learned on her journey to inspire others on stages such as TEDx and NAWBO. You'll find her on Instagram "gourmanding" her way around the globe, documenting her adventures on video, and dancing with her five grandkids.

www.mastermel.com

Get Your Shine On

Angel Marie Monachelli

My chronic pain is caused by a long list of conditions. I've been diagnosed with lupus, arthritis, and Sjögren's. And I dropped a microwave on my foot 30 years ago that damaged the ligaments. Sometimes the pain that suddenly comes out of nowhere will be so intense that it brings me to tears. My doctors don't even know how I'm getting a shoe on or walking around. Yet I am.

These medical conditions started showing up after I began to uncover several incidents of sexual abuse that I'd suppressed. When something's going on emotionally, it will come out physically. Your issues are in your tissues. Once I understood what was happening, I jumped into Reiki and used that universal life force energy to change the form of the energy. I quit beating myself up for allowing the abuse to happen. That belief didn't serve me anymore. I know no one will ever touch me like that again.

The healing was an internal process. It's all about energy and where your energy is focused.

When we come from a position of victimhood and step into that *woe-is-me place*, it brings us down lower and lower. It also brings us to a place where we are inactive and sit a lot. When we sit too much, our energy goes down even more. I learned how important it is to stand up every few minutes and bring that energy up.

Einstein declared that energy never dissolves. It merely changes form. So, when you change the form of the pain, and change the frequency of the vibration, you can release the pain.

Since I've gone through all of these immune-system diseases, I'm an expert now. I've spent over 20 years helping people to be able to go through pain and to be able to control their energy.

Our brain can only focus on one thing at a time. We think we can multitask, but we can't. So, when you're coming from a place of joy and focusing on appreciation rather than on the pain, you can shift your whole vibrational field away from the pain. I believe that *what you think about you bring about.* I don't want to be thinking about the pain.

I push the limits every day, every moment. To help alleviate pain and minimize my symptoms, I've made increasing positivity and joy my top priority.

Instead of focusing on something that takes me down or brings me pain, I think about what it is that motivates me. If it's taking my dog for a slow walk, okay. It's still a walk. I still do it. And that energizes me. That is exciting. Do whatever that is for you. It is so contagious when you bring up your energy.

When someone is pushing the limits, they're actually coming from the inside out. They're connecting and transforming what they see. They're changing their perspective and shifting the energy.

I have a few techniques for getting through the pain. I smile and laugh all the time. I just spontaneously start laughing. It's been scientifically proven that smiling and laughing change your energy.

There are two other very simple things that help, but we don't always remember to do them: drinking water and breathing deeply.

Why is water so important? Putting water in our bodies is like putting oil in an engine. If there isn't enough oil in an engine, it will seize up and stop. And so will your body. Water feeds your cells. It protects your joints. It helps your organs function. And it helps maintain your body temperature. It gets energy unstuck and moving through your body.

There was a time when I didn't think water was a big deal. Living in Phoenix, Arizona, in the desert, you need a lot of water. But I was drinking only sodas. All of a sudden, I had this severe pain. The doctor diagnosed kidney stones and said I got them because I didn't drink water. That was really a wakeup call. That's when I dove in and started studying about water. I gave up the soda and started drinking water—half of my body weight in ounces every day.

When you get the proper water intake, you'll have more clarity and focus, and you'll be more productive.

We breathe about 20,000 times a day, and we don't even think about it. When we consciously breathe deeply, we ignite our cells. We help oxygenize our body. We feel better and have more energy. Breathing deeply from your diaphragm raises your vibration and boosts your immune system.

One breathing tip I teach in my book is to take deep breaths every time you stop at a red light. Sit back, but don't close your eyes. Stay cognizant of what's going on around you. Put your hands on your belly and take several deep breaths. Waiting at a red light, you can usually get at least three in.

When you're drinking half your body weight in ounces of water, guess what? You're going to go to the bathroom a lot. So, while you're sitting there, or standing there, take some deep breaths. It's so easy to do. Put up a sign in your bathroom to remind yourself to BREATHE.

Take time for deep, diaphragmatic belly breathing. It will help you throughout your day to be in the moment, to calm your nerves, and to have more productivity, energy, and confidence.

I created the Shine On! Movement™ because I live it. I live it because I choose not to be a victim and live in pain. My responsibility, my drive, my inspiration, is to help you know that you don't have to be in pain. You can move through pain and change your energy.

Join the movement. Put more energy, joy, and positivity into all areas of your life. Raise your vibration. Shine On!

❊ ❊ ❊

Angel Marie Monachelli is an inspirational speaker, empowerment coach, TV host, and author of five national bestselling books including *Shine On!* She is the creator of the Shine On! Movement™ and the Elite Reiki Healing System™. For over 20 years, she has shared her Shine On! philosophy through her writing and speaking. As an event energy enhancer and fireball emcee, she brings the power of positive energy, engagement, and education to live and online events, helping presenters avoid Zoomed-out participants. She has been influential in the healing arts community in Phoenix for two decades. Her passion is teaching others how to experience the freedom of living their best lives with more energy, confidence, and joy.

www.angelmarieshines.com

Throw Perfectionism Out the Door

Karianne Munstedt

Believing in perfection has made life more difficult and confusing for so many women. We think we've got to show up perfect 100 percent of the time, and we hesitate to move forward until we think we can do it perfectly.

During my youth and young adult years, I was an overachiever striving for perfection in everything—my body, my appearance, my education, sports, marriage, homes, cars, jobs. What a burden. I looked like the perfectly put-together person on the outside, but on the inside, I was lost. I didn't know the authentic me. I did what I thought I was supposed to do without looking at the toll it took.

In my early 30s, I reconnected with my love of photography and picked up a camera again. While I still had my corporate job, I began to branch out and build my own photography business. As I started building my website, I realized I didn't have any pictures of myself I could use. *How could I be the face of my photography business and not put my face on my business?*

I barely existed in photos because of my fear of not being perfect and of being judged by others. All I could find were a few of me wearing a ball cap and an oversized T-shirt, or hiding behind someone else. My weight was the highest it had ever been. I didn't like how I looked, and I didn't want to be in a picture.

Something about being photographed amplifies our craving to have everything appear to be perfect—the perfect weight, the perfect hair, the perfect nails, and the perfect outfit. And I wasn't even close to my image of perfect.

When I arrived for my scheduled photo shoot, I hoped and prayed that I would be able to find at least one decent picture of myself to use online. All these negative voices inside my head were screeching full blast: *Kari, you're too fat to be photographed. Kari, who do you think you are for wanting to be photographed? This photographer doesn't even want to photograph you.*

In spite of showing up for the photo shoot riddled with fear and anxiety, I had the **very best time ever!** It was so much fun. The photographer made me feel so comfortable in front of the camera. As she guided me through the poses, I felt like the most beautiful person in the world. I left with my head held high and a new feeling of confidence.

When I looked at those beautiful photos, I wasn't seeing the Kari on the outside, I was seeing the Kari on the inside. I saw my soul reflected back at me. I saw who I was and who I was going to be someday.

When I was able to really see myself in those photos, it was life-changing. I felt empowered. I found the courage to be authentic and vulnerable. I had the self-assurance and the fuel to take that big leap forward to leave the security of my job and start my own business.

Wrenching ourselves free of that perfectionism notion, especially with our bodies, is a really hard thing. It hasn't been easy for me, but these are things that have worked. First, recognize that you hold this faulty belief. Notice what those voices in your head are saying. Are you constantly talking negatively to yourself without even noticing what you're doing? When you walk by a mirror do those critical voices say: *You're so fat. Your arms are too big. Your nose is too big.* Take a breath and acknowledge what those voices in your head are saying.

Then stop and reframe those negative thoughts as positive ones. My biggest concern has been my belly. I'd walk by a mirror and think: *Oh my gosh, my belly is huge. My clothes aren't fitting.* I've changed that to: *This belly is cushy. I gave birth to a baby out of this belly, and he likes to sleep on it.*

The change isn't going to happen overnight. But slowly, start taking one little step, then another little step, then another. Over time, you'll stop thinking that you have to be perfect. Dump the perfectionism myth. You're even more powerful when you are your real, authentic self.

Our bodies are the least interesting things about us. The most interesting things are what's in our minds and in our hearts. The things that make us unique are the things that people are interested in connecting with the most. That's what I show people through their photographs. I bring out the authentic self that wants to shine through. Giving that experience to other women motivates me to keep going.

It has taken me years on my spiritual journey to rid myself of the need to be perfect and to feel comfortable sharing my authentic self with the world. I want every woman to have that same experience I had. I want them to feel that same confidence and power to be authentic and real, and to make big leaps in their own lives.

So, let's take that perfectionism nonsense and throw it out the door!

Let's show up as our real selves, our true selves, with all our uniqueness. That's where we find our happiness. That's where we find the deepest connections. That's where we find love.

❋ ❋ ❋

Karianne Munstedt is an award-winning portrait photographer and business owner, speaker, coach, and author. She is an artist and nurturer who is fiercely motivated by using her talents to make women feel confident, empowered, and whole. As a curvy woman who was very critical of her body, she spent nearly a decade hiding behind the camera, never stepping in front of it out of fear of shame and judgment around her body and choices. Now, Karianne exists fully in photos for her business and in her personal life. She routinely posts real and raw photos of herself, shifting the way we define beauty and proving that we all are worthy of existing fully in photos, no matter our perceived flaws. Karianne inspires women around the world to show up as real versions of themselves in their photos, not the "perfect" versions they were taught to show. #realisthenewperfect

www.kariannemunstedt.com

From Fistfights to Beauty Pageants

Lesley Nardini

While I was in grade school, my parents divorced, and I found myself moving around a lot. My mother struggled as a single parent and had a hard time providing structure and guidance for five kids. My life became chaos. Feeling a lot of anger and loneliness, I turned into a tomboy who got in a lot of fistfights. That was my defense mechanism. I wasn't the sweet, pretty girl playing by the rules. I didn't want to put on dresses. I was an angry rebel.

People reacted to that persona—not in a positive way—and it started to shape how I saw myself. But when I got to junior high and started being interested in boys, I began changing my image and being more feminine. I put myself together differently—with mixed success.

I was that kid who wanted to be involved with things. So, I tried out for every single thing that came around—dance team, cheerleading, drill team, flag carrier, student government. I tried out for everything—and was picked for nothing.

During my senior year in high school, I tried out for a beauty pageant. I thought I had a good chance of getting one of 20 available slots since there were only 30 girls trying out. When I wasn't picked—again—I thought, *That's it, I'm done. I never get picked for anything. I quit!* But one of the 20 girls dropped out, and I was number 21. You would have thought I'd won the Miss Universe Pageant, I was so excited! It was through this experience that I got my first taste of the incredible world of pageants.

Being in that pageant did so much for my self-esteem. It built my confidence. They taught us how to hold ourselves, how to polish ourselves up and present ourselves well, and how that can go a long way in life. It was absolutely magical. I loved everything about it.

For the talent presentation I made up a jazz dance to the theme from the *Pink Panther*. I worked on it all on my own in my living room. No professional help. No professional training.

Standing backstage getting ready to go out and perform that dance, I started thinking: *What have I done? This is going to be a disaster. I have no idea if this is any good.* I felt terrified. I wanted to run home and quit because it was so hard. I felt like my head was going to burst off the top of my body at any second. But as I stood there, a different phrase came in my mind, *I can do this.* I kept saying that over and over and over to myself—*I can do this, I can do this, I can do this*—till I actually felt confident.

That was a pivotal moment in my life where I realized that telling myself *I can do this* gave me courage and confidence. Still to this day, if I'm experiencing fear about something, I stop myself and say, *I can do this.* I give myself that little burst of *I've got this*!

I continue to push through failure and disappointment and setbacks. I've accomplished a lot of what I have been able to achieve because of my mindset and sheer determination to not ever give up. That's the key to having anything you want in life—stick with it and don't let failure one, failure two, or failure three be a reason to not continue on to get what you really want in life.

Participating in pageants taught me another valuable lesson. **You** get to decide how you feel about yourself. **You** get to choose your thoughts and your feelings. You do not have to let other people or past experiences or society or social media tell you what you ought to look like or what you ought to think about yourself. You get to choose your own thoughts around that.

It sounds simple. It is simple. But simple does not always mean easy. Because we get conditioned to think a certain way, it takes effort to learn how to think about ourselves in a new way.

Success has come by changing my mindset. Learning to create a mindset with a healthy, positive outlook on life, on other people, and on ourselves, is the same process as getting physically fit and healthy. It does not happen magically by accident.

When I want to become physically fit and healthy, I'm going to put in the work. That requires goal setting, learning the steps, taking action, and having another person push me to stay on that path. Once I get physically fit and healthy, I can't just check that off my list. I still have to work at it. It's a lifelong process that becomes easier the more I do it.

Having a healthy, positive, and optimistic mindset is the same process—set your goals, learn the steps, and get help. Take action on a regular basis that keeps you moving in the direction of your dreams and goals. If you let up and say, *Okay, I'm a healthy, optimistic person now, I don't have to work on it anymore,* it's easy to slide back into cynicism and pessimism and all those things that take our lives in a downward spiral.

Once you have that mindset and understand that concept, it's easier to push away outside influences and unproductive thoughts. No more excuses: *Oh, my life is not great because of X, and because of Y, and because of the government, and because of my parents.* When you take responsibility for the success of your life, all those things drop away.

Empowerment is learning how to choose your own thoughts instead of being a victim. It's learning how to build your confidence so that you value who you are as a person. It's creating your life instead of reacting to life. That puts you in control. Success happens when you stick to it. When you have that confidence, that belief, that ability to choose your thoughts on a daily basis, then you have the ability to mold your life, and choose the life you want for yourself.

✵ ✵ ✵

Lesley Nardini is an award-winning international speaker, bestselling author, image consultant, coach, customer service expert, and a newly licensed real estate agent in California. She has spoken to thousands of people around the world, including Fortune 500 companies in 45 US states and several countries. Her acclaimed books include *It's Not About Customer Service, It's All About Personal Touch* and *Keys to a Winning Attitude, 26 Ways to Have a Positive Mindset.* She has gone from being an awkward, insecure teenager to a pageant competitor and winner many times over. Lesley was crowned Ms. World Elite when she was 58. At the age of 60, she competed with women aged 45 and over to win the title of Mrs. Classique USA 2021. For her, participating in pageants at this stage of life helps her stay mentally and physically fit, and gives her the opportunity to inspire women of all ages with her message that beauty and vibrancy have no expiration date. She is looking forward to competing for the title of Mrs. Classique Globe in 2022.

www.lesleynardini.com

A Geek Who Can Speak

TK O'Geary

When I was new in my career, a lot of what I was doing in the workforce was running different types of analyses to help the company leadership determine what action to take. Because I was a mathematician fascinated with numbers and analysis, I thought everybody wanted to know about all the calculations and how we got to those final answers. So, in my presentations, I exuberantly dumped a ton of data on my unfortunate coworkers.

One day, a couple of coworkers who had seen me present, stopped me in the hallway. After politely asking if I had a moment, one of them said, "I've got to tell you, when you present your reports in the meetings, we don't listen to you." *Well, okay,* I thought. To me, failure is opportunity to understand data. "Really?" I questioned, "Why not?" They replied, "Well, it takes too long." They started going into a few other things, but all I heard was, *"It takes too long."* In my mind, I quickly came up with a very simple solution to the problem—*I'll speak faster.*

And they still didn't listen. Failure Opportunity Number Two. Not only was I boring them with an overload of data, now I was doing it even faster. It was horrible.

I could not read an audience. I had no idea people were tuning out. I thought people were looking down because they were taking notes. *Isn't this great? People are so engaged. They're writing down all these cool calculations and information about which test we used.* No, they were not. Completely wrong. Complete failure. I was clueless.

I would never have gone anywhere in my career if hadn't learned how to communicate effectively. I am so grateful that a technical writer in the company tricked me into going to a Toastmaster meeting. I was excited when she invited me to lunch. I knew she was a great cook, and that she had gotten a new bread-making machine for Christmas. "I've been doing some things with the bread-making machine and pulled some of the vegetables from my garden. Why don't I make lunch for us?" She even tempted me with my favorite—brownies with nuts.

As we walked to the conference room for "lunch," I felt like this little puppy following her thinking, *This is going to be soooo good.* When she opened the door, instead of lunch, there was a timing device and Toastmaster's banner. My mind raced. *I don't need this. I just need to run my numbers for the analysis. I don't need to talk to people. I just need to calculate. I'm fine.* I frowned at her and said, "I know what this is." And this very persuasive woman said, "You need this. Sit down."

By the end of the meeting, I realized that she was absolutely correct. I could not judge what an audience was doing. I spoke way too fast. I didn't have a path for the audience to follow. I was all over the place.

She—and Toastmasters—changed my career path and my life. I'm forever thankful that they took that nerd and geek side of me and taught me how to communicate effectively.

After learning everything I could from Toastmasters for a year and a half, I started getting asked to lead projects and teams. Then I started getting promoted. Being the analyst, I paid attention to why I was getting promoted. Nearly every single time I got a promotion, somebody mentioned my ability to communicate. My newly developed skills helped me as I moved higher and higher in leadership positions.

Along the way, I earned a nickname. People forgot my name,

but they would say, "Hey, could you go get that geek who can speak?" Today, I proudly wear that moniker, A Geek Who Can Speak.

Speaking was a career that was the farthest thing from what I ever thought I'd do. While I was in veterinary school in college, my dad brought a statistician from the Air Force base home for dinner. Over a two-hour conversation with him, I discovered my hidden fascination with data, and quickly changed my major to math and statistics.

I also discovered that I have an ability to empathize with people—an odd proficiency for a nerd. As a Lean Six Sigma Master Black Belt, I look at the people side of process improvement. I want people to succeed. When I can help improve a process, or help a leader find a way to connect, that to me is a good day.

During more than 30 years in Toastmasters, I've learned communication and leadership skills that have helped me advance in my career as a mathematician and analyst in STEM fields.

As a speaking coach, I help people who aren't professional speakers get up and speak about their organization or to their organization.

I had the privilege of helping a physician who was asked to give the keynote for her state's governor's prayer breakfast. Instead of a dull, factual speech, we used a few stories based on her experiences, and put together an absolutely powerful 20-minute talk. She delivered the speech perfectly to an audience of several hundred people and received a standing ovation. After her speech, the line of people waiting to talk to her was a long one. I felt like a proud mom seeing her connect with an audience that was not her typical audience while conveying such a compelling message. That moment of pride for someone else's accomplishment—it fuels my engine.

It's been quite a journey from that clueless nerd who thought communication was dumping lots of data on my unfortunate coworkers to a certified world-class speaking coach. The help I received, even when I didn't know I needed help, has come full circle as I help people become more successful by improving their communication skills. I never in my life thought I'd ever be where I am today. Never. And it's what I live for.

❋ ❋ ❋

TK O'Geary is known as a geek who can speak and lead. She has a bachelor's degree in mathematics (computer science, statistics), an MBA, and is a Lean Six Sigma Master Black Belt. As a process excellence consultant and certified world-class speaking coach, she has coached hundreds of TED speakers and diverse professionals to become stronger communicators and leaders. With over 30 years in Toastmasters, she is a Distinguished Toastmaster (DTM), Toastmasters International Board Member, and Toastmasters Distinguished District Director. In 2020, she received the distinction as an Albuquerque First Woman of Influence. TK is a board member and past president of an organization that helps youth increase science, technology, engineering, and math knowledge and leadership skills.

www.dtmtko.com
www.tkogeary.com

Crowdsourcing Miracles

Michelle Patterson

Ninety days to live—that was the death sentence my doctor handed me on April 15, 2019, if I didn't start chemotherapy. I chose to treat my stage IV breast cancer diagnosis using cannabis protocols instead.

Before that day, I had been so other-focused for so long that I lost myself. I would do these massive events, like North America's largest women's conference. Instead of coming home and resting when one was finished, I went on to the next huge project, and then the next. I had been under all this immense stress.

Through this diagnosis, my body was communicating with me: *Have fun. Stop trying to be everything and do everything. Do your genius. Do your wheelhouse. Be that consummate cheerleader. Be that promoter.*

During a particularly stressful time in our family right before my diagnosis, my husband showed me Jordan Peterson's book *12 Rules for Life*. Rule #2 was, "Treat yourself like somebody you're responsible for helping." He looked at me and said, "Michelle, you need to treat yourself like somebody you're responsible for."

When I got the diagnosis a few days later, it hit me hard. I had taken care of everyone else since I was seven, but I never really took care of myself. This diagnosis gave me the opportunity to love on myself, to really show up for myself, and to treat myself like somebody I'm responsible for.

The doctor used fear tactics to convince me to do chemo. I chose not to live in fear. I made a choice then, and I continue to choose today, to show up in love and to bring 100 percent joy into all aspects of my life and healing.

During my wellness journey, I put together my Wellness Team Family (WTF) consisting of doctors and wellness providers who were willing to collaborate. We created The Real Share, a collaborative online community of medical professionals and patients who've gone through their own medical journeys. Individually, we don't have all the answers, but collectively we absolutely do.

We're having honest "kitchen-table" conversations where we share our first-hand experiences and resources so people can make the best choice for themselves. No stigmas. No fear tactics. Nobody's telling you that you have 90 days to live. That's not anyone else's decision. You get to decide what resonates with you. It's your choice. It's you owning your own wellness.

Through The Real Share, we're joining geniuses to give and receive support, and crowdsourcing miracles.

I take on the role I'm good at. I'm a team builder. I'm a promoter. I'm a cheerleader. I put the team together that is able to accomplish the goal of the project.

A lot of times when people create teams and partnerships like this, they're not really clear about where it's going to go. I've learned to be very deliberate about how I want to show up and what I want.

Here's what I do.

Before going into a meeting or negotiation or starting any project with someone else, I sit down by myself, and spend 15 minutes writing out on one page what it is that I want to come out of that situation using my SOS formula:

1. **Show up**. I get centered and decide how I want to show up. How does my genius complement your genius? How can we create magic together?

2. **Obstacles**. What obstacles are we going to face? Where do I want this to go?

3. **Steps**. What are the next steps to put in place? What do I want to create? What follow-through is needed?

When I plan it out in its entirety so that I am crystal clear on what I want and how I can serve others, it's the difference between playing all out 100 percent or not.

Here's an example of how this played out for me.

As I was creating The Real Share, people were coming to the table, myself included, where we oftentimes didn't know exactly what those needs were. I decided I needed to have a needs-assessment tool. So, I sat down and meditated with clear intentions: *What I'm looking for is somebody that has an ability to do assessments. I want them to be a clinical psychologist. I want them to have a PhD because I want to have the science behind the assessment.*

My producer had set up a Zoom call for after my meditation that afternoon. All I knew was this person's name was Richard and he could help me with The Real Share. I opened up our conversation with, "Richard, tell me about your background and more about you." He said, "I'm a PhD, a clinical psychologist, and my company does assessments." Just like that, Dr. Richard Schuster showed up in my life.

That's the kind of stuff that happens when you get very specific. You can reach out to the Universe and manifest miracles instantly.

Up until my diagnosis, I felt like I was always three feet from gold. I had the mindset that the Universe was helping me, but it wasn't totally on my side. Now, with how intentional I am with everything I do, I feel quite the opposite. The Universe is absolutely working directly with me to create wellness for me and the community.

That's one blessing that I've gotten from this diagnosis—that skill set of being able to get very intentional about the teams that I'm putting together and the work that I'm doing. And lo and behold, the people that are the right fit in that space are showing up.

I've gotten very, very particular about who I allow to play on my playground. I'm playing a very big game. The people I run with won't settle for anything less than playing all out.

I'm going through this process of a pain-free cancer because individuals have shared their personal experiences of what worked for them.

In 2020, I celebrated turning 50, a birthday I was told I would never see. I still have cancer, yet I'm filled with joy. I don't have the pain. I don't have the heartache. I don't have the fear. I'm living every moment, manifesting miracles, and helping other people manifest theirs.

Michelle Patterson is the chief experience officer of The Real Share, and a leading advocate for modern, holistic health and wellness. She hosts *The Real Share Huddle and Podcast*. For 10 years, she served as the president of the California Women's Conference, the nation's largest and longest-running conference for women in North America. Michelle founded the Global Women Foundation Network, a community of over a million. The author of *Women Change the World*, she is a sought-after media commentator for Bloomberg, CNBC, Fox Business News, ESPN, and HuffPost. In 2016, Ms. Patterson was presented with a lifetime achievement award by President Barack Obama and the Corporation for National and Community Service for her lifelong commitment to building a stronger nation through service.

www.therealshare.com

Who Do You Think You Are?

Tamara Patzer

While working on my programs and podcasting, I was feeling very discombobulated, a little off. I kept hearing that little voice saying, *Who do you think you are?*

And I'm thinking to myself, *Why is this voice bugging me about who do I think I am? Where did that come from? Everything I'm doing is based on my education, or I'm sharing what I've already done successfully. What happened that my subconscious is trying to bring up?*

I paid attention to that voice and memories started surfacing.

In Sunday school when I was four years old, I was singing the way a little kid would sing—exuberantly at the top of my lungs. "Jesus loves me this I know, for the Bible tells me so." I was so happy. And I was told, "Shut up. You can't sing."

In the third grade, I'm supposed to sing "Twinkle, twinkle little star." I can still see the piano the choir teacher was playing in this little room. Well, I don't know the song. I know four words, "Twinkle, twinkle little star," but that's about it. The teacher starts playing the piano and I sing, "Twinkle, twinkle little star." She stops me saying, "No, you can't sing. You can't be in the chorus."

In high school I won a scholarship to visit Thailand. I can still see one of my so-called best friends standing on my front porch, her mom's station wagon parked at the curb, telling me she thought another girl should have gotten the scholarship, not me.

Decades later, this guy named Anthony was helping me write a song called "The Messenger's Messenger." Sitting across from me and playing his guitar, he says, "Okay, just sing what I sing." And so I did. He goes, "Yeah, that's **good**. You're an alto." I didn't even know what an alto was. He told me I could be trained to sing.

I did not sing from the third grade, where I was nine years old, until I was 60. All those years, I just mouthed the words when I was in church or any place I had to sing.

All of us have some moment in time where we were told, "No, you cannot speak. Little children are seen and not heard." Or, "You're not good enough to let your voice be heard." Or a friend tells you, "You shouldn't have won." Remember that moment?

Until I became aware of these moments that were lodged in my subconscious, I never understood why it is so important to me that I help other people be heard and seen. Now, it all makes perfect sense why my purpose in life is helping people find their voice—it's because somebody told me my voice should not be heard. Somebody told me I couldn't sing. Somebody told me I wasn't good enough.

There comes a time where something inside of us surfaces and we start to rebel. *Well, I'm going to do it anyway*! Now, if I really want to sing, I can go take voice lessons and I will be okay.

When those negative, nagging "who-do-you-think-you-are" voices show up, thank them. Ask yourself what's happening that you're doubting who you are. Dig for those stories from your past. Look for insights like I had about my singing.

Those voices in my head turned out to be a little prompting on something I needed to create to help my clients start finding their voice, writing their books, and creating their bigger authority footprint. Those voices helped me find my purpose.

Everything I've done in my whole life has been all about communication. I started young when my mom was a writer. I used to interview her on my little cassette player pretending she was a famous *New York Times* bestselling author.

I see myself as the messenger's messenger. I interview people on podcasts so they can tell their story. I do everything I can to make them look good, and make sure they're the superstar on one of my shows.

When you look back, situations may seem negative. But your subconscious is saying, *Hey, pay attention to this because this could help you become whoever you're supposed to become.*

Come up with an inventory of all the good things you've done. Take a "who-do-I-think-I-am" inventory—an inventory of your expertise and your authority. Set a timer for 15 minutes and dump out all the good things you've done that you've gotten recognition or accolades for. Maybe you won an art contest. Maybe you're a singer. Maybe you have a certificate or a license. What are your gifts and talents? Write them all down. Don't leave anything out. You never know what they might mean later on.

Acknowledge what you've accomplished. Once you've done that, you'll have a really good foundation to build from. Start by recognizing that you have a big message and big mission. Claim who you are and what your purpose is. Find your voice, and then tell the world.

You are exactly the person you're supposed to be. You'll keep getting better and better, especially when you start asking yourself, *Who do I think I am?*

❋ ❋ ❋

Tamara "Tami" Patzer is the CEO and founder of Women Innovators Publishing and Media, bestselling author, international speaker, and a former editor and member of the Pulitzer-prize-nominated Sun Coast Media Group news team. She is the creator of Florida Gulf Coast University's Social Media certification program, and is a frequent social media expert guest on TV news programs across the nation on ABC, NBC, CBS, Fox, and CW. She has shared her message at Harvard Faculty Club, NASDAQ, Coco-Cola, and Microsoft. Tami hosts *Women Innovators Radio Network, Optimal Health Radio*, and *The Thought Leaders* show on The Business Innovators Network on iHeart Radio. She helps her clients share their big messages and big missions through book publishing, social media, and mass media exposure.

www.tamipatzer.com
www.dailysuccessinstitute.com

Facing Life Head On

Carey Portell

A few days after my 35ᵗʰ birthday 10 years ago, two of my children and I were hit by a drunk driver who died at the scene. I was severely injured. I needed multiple surgeries—three in the first 10 days, and seven the first two years, plus lots of therapy. Thankfully my children were less severely injured.

The doctors told me that if I ever walked again, it would be minimal. They said I would probably be totally reliant on a wheelchair in eight to 10 years. Four years after the accident, I recovered to "partially disabled" status. Nine years after the accident, I had my 13ᵗʰ surgery. They were right about the wheelchair.

Before the accident, I had been very active raising our four kids and working our farm. I was a person who was not used to just sitting still—until **that** life came to a complete halt.

For a long time, the only thing I could do was heal. My goal in the first few years was to be able to walk.

It took a long time to recover from each surgery. I dreaded going through the recovery and healing period. Each time, I had to mentally barter with myself. *Okay, this is going to make it better. If I want to walk, I need to go through this again.*

Between the anesthesia and the pain medicines, the first two years were almost like a movie trailer. I don't remember a whole lot. It was so difficult for me to be cognizant. I can pick parts out of my memories, but not the whole thing. It was incredibly challenging to be down and healing so slowly.

The first time I was able to stand up by myself and get my own bowl out of the cabinet, I called my husband to celebrate. It was unbelievable!

Unfortunately for my family, those first two years were solely about me, just getting me up and in a wheelchair where I could do stuff. Even though I couldn't help it, I have mom guilt about those years of not being able to concentrate more on my children.

You need to have a motivator, a driving force, behind whatever you're going to do. Everybody says, "What is your *why?*" It's starting to become cliché, but it's so true. What is your driving force? What is your motivation to get to your end goal? When you want to quit, ask yourself, *Why am I doing this in the first place? What was my passion at the beginning of this goal? What drove me to want to do this so badly, to make this whole plan to get to this goal?* Remind yourself of what your motivation is.

My husband and my children were my motivation from the beginning. I didn't give up. I felt if I did, that would give my children permission to give up when they faced adversity in their lives. I could not give them that permission. If they saw that Mom didn't give up, then they would know they can't give up either.

Now, every other person on this planet has become my motivation for speaking and writing about my experience. I take that same philosophy to anyone who is willing to listen and learn from what I've gone through. I encourage them to make choices to start thriving instead of just surviving. I want to inspire people to believe in themselves enough to have the courage and motivation to overcome whatever adversity they have. I want them to look at me and say, "Well, I CAN do this."

I don't always know if I'm reaching people. At one of my son's ballgames, another mom came over to talk to me. Everything with her was so negative. I kept trying to end the conversation because I could not let her negativity drag me down. I still wasn't strong enough. When I turned to leave, she put her hand on my shoulder, and I thought, *What now?* I turned back to see tears in her eyes. "Carey, you don't understand. The things that you write in your blog and that you say on Facebook, they're helping me so much. I have so much anger, and I don't know where it comes from. But you give me the motivation each week to try to be better, to try harder at my life." Time stopped for me. *Wow, so people really are hearing what I'm saying.*

That's why I'm doing this—for all those silent people out there who are suffering in silence. They may not have the same challenges I do, but it's the same process to get through any challenge—believe in yourself.

Even though I had to be strong as a young child, I really didn't see myself as strong, and I didn't believe in myself. Going through the last 10 years, I have come to understand I was strong from the very beginning. I had no idea how strong I was.

There's no success that does not come with challenges. When you know in your heart what you're doing is right, and you know where you want to go, find the courage and the grit to keep plowing through to do what you know you need to do. Tell yourself, *This is my focus. Nothing's going to deter me. I know what I'm going to do.*

At this point in my life, I have every confidence in myself that I can do anything I want to. I know in my heart that if I put my mind to it, I can figure out anything. And I know you can too.

❈ ❈ ❈

Carey Portell is a national speaker and cattle farmer in Missouri. She speaks to audiences across the United States, sharing her inspiring story of being beautifully broken, shattering barriers, and thriving with disabilities. She demonstrates that attitude changes everything by consistently choosing a positive perspective despite her pain and deteriorating disabilities. Carey advocates for AgrAbility, an organization that has guided her to continue farming despite her handicaps. She recently published the bestseller, *Facing Life Head On,* in which she authentically shares the story of her recovery.

www.careyportell.com

Don't Tell Me I Can't

Lillian Robinson

I can't stand to hear anyone tell me, "No, you can't." I know that there's a way to get anything done, and I'll figure out a way to do it, thank you. I was the middle child and the only girl in a house full of boys. So, whenever I heard, "No, you can't," I wanted to know why not? I was **that** child.

When I was in third grade, I had a serious injury and was in a full cast. The doctor told my grandmother, "She's never going to walk again. She'll always have limitations in everything she will do." My grandmother glared at him and said, "I'm not even going to hear that."

But I believed what the doctor said. I was so distraught over that injury and what had happened to me that I had given up. But my grandmother knew that I had a lot more in me than I knew I had. Every day she was my physical therapist.

She started me on a regimen of getting back to walking.

I didn't get a free pass. She made me get up and walk. I had to do everything like my brothers. "No one is going to bring you anything. If you want to eat, you need to get up and walk to the table. If you want to go outside, you need to take yourself outside. No one is going to carry you. You need to do this for yourself."

I argued with her. "Why not? I'm a kid. I'm hurt. Why can't my brothers wait on me?" That got me nowhere. So, I fed myself. I got up and went to school. I did everything she told me.

My incredible grandmother wanted me to know, "If you don't do these things, this is going to shape the rest of your life." That motivated me to do the things I needed to do. Now, was it easy? No, it was very painful. But it taught me that my limitations are the ones that I put on myself. I learned not to give up.

Even though the doctor said I would never walk again, I was able to join the Air Force. I pushed through all the different physical types of rigorous, military training. And I made it through, thanks to my grandmother pushing me.

Throughout my career, I haven't always done everything the traditional or conventional way. I always find a way to get around obstacles and get things done. When I see a roadblock or an obstacle to my destiny, I decide, *This is where I want to go. Now how do I get there?* So, if it means I have to push and feel a little friction while I'm moving things around, that's what I do. That's who I am.

If we only stay in our comfortable rut doing the easy things, we'll never get to that next level.

One way I stay out of that comfortable rut is to surround myself with people who are not always going to tell me I did a good job. Those are the people that, throughout my career, were the toughest on me and were not always my biggest fans—like an instructor I had when I started my doctoral program.

In my first class, my instructor said, "You know what, you need to drop this class. You're not going to make it through this program. You just don't have the skills. You can't write." I was taken aback by all these negative things she had to say to me. She was the instructor. Wasn't the instructor supposed to be encouraging me? Then the thought struck me: *Did she just tell me I can't do this? Here we go again! Somebody's telling me I can't do something.*

That was what I needed at that time. Telling me, "You can't," made me want to do it even more.

I also remembered my grandmother's words: "If you don't

do these things, this is going to shape the rest of your life." I stayed in the class. I stayed in the program. I knew I'd be okay.

What if I had listened to that instructor and not completed the program? Getting my doctorate was a part of my destiny that got me to where I am now. It's an important part of the teaching and training that I'm doing. Without it, I would not have had some of the success I've had in my life.

I had all kinds of excuses that could have kept me from doing what I was created to do—Black woman from the south who grew up with nothing. I am so grateful for the people in my life who pushed me to make positive changes.

I chose mentors in my life who didn't look like me and who weren't like me. I wanted mentors who had different life experiences that could bring something to the table that I never thought about before. I wanted people who were not going to tell me exactly what I wanted to hear. I wanted to hear the truth even when it was not easy to hear.

I'm sure my grandmother would be amazed if she could see Dr. Lillian Robinson the teacher standing in front of people from all over the country, doing what she did so many years ago in a little one-room school. When she was 13 years old, she started her life-long career by teaching African American veterans that couldn't read or write. It's very emotional for me to even think about the sacrifices she made and know they were not in vain. I would love to have her walk through the door and see what that little nine-month-old baby she took in and raised is doing now.

Nobody makes it to where they want to get without someone helping them get there. As you push the limits, remember you're being pushed up by other people who will lift you up to where you need to go.

❋ ❋ ❋

Dr. Lillian Robinson is the training and employee engagement manager for the US Bureau of Land Management (BLM) for Arizona and New Mexico. She travels around the country providing training, coaching, and mentoring for employees, managers, and supervisors. She is a member of the New Mexico Executive Management Team and the Arizona State Leadership Team where she is the only African American woman on either team. As the advisor for the Retention, Engagement, Diversity, and Inclusion team for Arizona, she is responsible for ensuring all employees are treated fairly and are appreciated for what each one brings to the BLM. Before joining BLM, Lillian served her country for 22 years as an Air Force (AF) member. She completed her AF career as one of the top education and training managers assigned to the 56th Fighter Squadron at Luke Air Force Base. She has a master's degree in human resource management and a PhD in adult and postsecondary education. She is an adjunct professor at several local universities. Lillian has dedicated her life to making a difference in the lives of others through education and training.

Email: LRobinson42@cox.net

Whose Voice Are You Listening To?

Sandra Dee Robinson

We are not born with self-doubt. We're born whole and designed for greatness. We are conceived with all of that in place. But as we go through life, we allow certain things to come in that create self-doubt. I allowed what my mother told me to create that self-doubt in me.

My mother started reprograming me before I was even born. Her unhappiness that she was pregnant had a detrimental energetic effect on me. She wanted me to believe that life would be better if I hadn't been born. Those were the actual words that came out of her mouth.

For a long time, I believed those words. I grew up not knowing that I had a voice of my own.

Acting was my safe haven. I spent years studying human behavior, body language, psychology, and why people react the way they do. I used that knowledge to step into the world of the characters I played. And I used acting to avoid the toxic feelings I harbored from growing up with my mother.

All I knew about myself was that I had a talent to be somebody else. I played all my cards on that acting talent. There was no Plan B. I had no understanding of my value outside that of being an actor. I wasn't even comfortable talking to strangers.

I won the Miss Pennsylvania title by putting on the character of a pageant winner. I studied the pageant girls—how they moved, what they did, what they said, and what it would look like to win—and then did that.

When I started acting in daytime soaps, I was so uncomfortable with fans walking up to me that I ran away from them. I didn't think I was worthy. Fans would wait outside the studio to get pictures and autographs from the cast, but I would sneak out the back. I was too afraid they would see that I wasn't anything special.

Once, our whole cast helped raise money for a children's charity. As we all stood on stage at the event, I hid myself behind other cast members. I was good there. When one of the most gregarious actors suddenly stuck a microphone in my face and said, "Say something," my mind went completely blank. I didn't actually pass out, but I have no idea what I said. I couldn't handle doing something like that without putting on a character.

Now I teach people to find their voice, to find their strength, and to communicate in the most natural, authentic way. But the fact is, I had none of that back then. I wanted to be told what to do and how to be. I felt safe only when I was delving into a character.

People would say, "Good job," and I'd get a paycheck. That validated me. But when I hosted an event or was interviewed, I didn't know how to act. Once, when I was being interviewed to host an infomercial, the director handed me a microphone and said "Oh, sweetie, just be yourself," I literally blacked out. I had nothing in that Sandra Dee file. Nothing.

I had this sense of anger and frustration—*Why is it that other people can talk in front of groups, and talk to strangers, and have a laugh in a conversation? They're fine, while I hide in the corner.*

I had been listening to the voice in my head: *Who do you think you are? Nobody's going to listen to you. You don't have enough education. You don't have enough connections. You don't have enough!"* I had to realize whose voice it was that was talking to me. It wasn't mine, and I guarantee it wasn't God's.

It took years of personal work before I recognized that the programming I got from my mother was wrong. Something rooted deep inside started to surface and helped me stop owning the bullying I got from her. I started to put some of these pieces together and uncover my authentic core.

One of the first times I got up in front of a crowd as myself was to raise money for a tiny animal sanctuary in South Jersey. They rescue animals that come from illegal exotic-pet trades and traveling zoos or that are dumped when people that buy odd animals don't want them anymore.

In this little zoo, each of these animals has a plaque that explains their story. Kids would point at a monkey because half of its body had been burned by an abusive former zookeeper. Through stories like that, children, and adults as well, learned lessons about compassion, understanding, and acceptance.

Because this cause meant so much to me, I was able to call strangers and get them involved. I'm talking about strangers that are celebrities—like some of the folks from Saturday Night Live. I bussed them down from New York on a school bus for a fund raiser. Oh, this was not glamorous. But these celebrities came and gave their time and raised enough money to support the zoo for an entire year.

When I got up on stage at that fund raiser, I was doing something that was close to my heart and reflected my values. It wasn't about me. I was able to be the authentic Sandra Dee, not a character I had studied. It lit me up!

It wasn't difficult to speak as my authentic self because the cause was so important to me. It connected with my authentic core and my values: my love of animals, my need to teach, and my connection to nature and God. It all started to come together for me. It was such a personal accomplishment.

Growing up, I didn't have a voice at all. And now, I'm just the opposite. I speak up for what I believe in, and I encourage other people to speak up for what they believe in. I'm an introvert, and yet I'm an international speaker. You can throw me in front of a crowd of thousands and I'm excited, but I'm not terrified.

There were certain gifts that I had forgotten I had. I had dismissed them or hidden them because of what my mother wanted me to believe. When I remembered these gifts and passions were part of my authentic core, I started to pull them back out.

I left acting when I didn't feel like what I did had a direct effect helping people. But my acting career did give me a platform that I have been able to leverage when I finally learned to find my voice and use it. I'm grateful that the recognition I have opens doors. I love working directly with people and helping them find their voice, tap into what they are designed to do, and manifest their impact in the world.

Don't believe the voices that are telling you lies about yourself. Don't let them stop you from finding your voice and speaking out. When you discover your authentic core and you connect with your passions and values, everything becomes easier and faster. You can be who you really are.

❁ ❁ ❁

Sandra Dee Robinson had a successful decades-long career in television with starring roles in *Another World, The Bold and Beautiful, General Hospital,* and *Days of Our Lives,* plus guest roles on *CSI Miami, Criminal Minds, Two and a Half Men,* and others. In 2010 she founded Charisma on Camera. As a performance coach, she works with business owners, experts, and celebrities to perfect their presentation and on-camera skills earning her the nickname of The Charisma Coach. Her Horsepowered Consulting business offers specialized equine-assisted coaching programs. Sandra Dee has had many titles— actress, author, TV host, podcast host, international speaker, trainer, and dog and horse fanatic. Her other title is "wife" to a renowned Hollywood stuntman. (Never a dull moment around their house.) Her mission is to illuminate the path for people to fully express all they are *Designed* to be.

www.sandradeerobinson.com

The Power of Words

Cali Rossen

People are always curious about the name of my company: POW Girl Productions. *POW* represents what I strongly believe—the Power of Words.

Words are powerful—the words others say to us, and the words we say to ourselves. It's important to be careful which words you believe are true. In my early life, I believed words that held me back, words that made me believe I didn't fit in.

My parents split up when I was a toddler, and I lived with my mom. When my father showed up on the doorstep, he was usually drunk. And my mom was usually freaking out. I was still learning language and words, and didn't understand everything they said, but I recognized the negative feelings and harsh energy of those words.

I knew something was wrong. In the back of my mind, I kept playing those words, *Something's wrong, something's wrong.* That thread has run through my whole life pretty much— *Something's wrong.*

Around the same time, I had to undergo EEGs. I didn't know why they were testing my brain impulses, but my mom told me I was having seizures. I don't remember that. But I do remember being in the doctor's office several times. To me, that was definite proof something was wrong—**with me.**

When I was held back a year in kindergarten, I colored in

more of that picture. *Something is definitely wrong with me—I'm not smart.*

I had proof something was wrong with me because of the tests. I had proof that I was not smart because I was being held back. That was my reality.

I had barely-passing grades through elementary school and junior high. I knew I was stupid.

When I was in my teens, my mom remarried, and we moved to Texas. The first week in my new high school, I had a meeting with the dean of girls, Mrs. Wheeler. As we were finishing the meeting, she looked at me and said, "You're going to be somebody someday. I just know it."

Her words created a new potential in me that shifted my mindset completely. Changing my thoughts about myself changed my actions.

I got straight As and was on the honor roll. I was chosen to be on the school dance team, and I performed routines at halftime at the football games. In college, I was a straight-A student. I graduated magna cum laude and became a member of Phi Theta Kappa International Honor Society.

I thrived!

I changed my mindset and my life that quickly because of those few words Mrs. Wheeler said to me.

But in life, people aren't always going to say those things we need to hear. So, we've got to practice saying those things to ourselves.

Recently, I was looking in the mirror, and I thought, *Gosh, you're looking kind of heavy.* And then I go, *Hold on, let me change my mind.* So, I closed my eyes and said, *Mind, come on. You are beautiful. You are gorgeous.* When I opened my eyes, I literally appeared different to myself.

Words are powerful. What do you want to be? What do you tell yourself? Which words are you going to nurture and let grow? Choose the ones that nurture your best self.

I do my best to keep my mind in PST—Positive Self-Talk. The words from a song I used to play over and over and over have stayed with me for years: "I am a promise. I am a possibility. I am a great big bundle of potentiality." Those words are how I feel about myself. One of the last things my mom said to me before passing was, "You can be anything you want." She reinforced that bundle of potentiality within me.

Because I thought I was stupid, I've been doing things all my life to prove that I'm not. I have nothing to prove. The only thing any of us have to prove is love. The true connection with people is what really matters.

You have the power within you that promises unimaginable potentiality. Empower yourself with your words.

※ ※ ※

Cali T. Rossen is a Voice Arts Awards nominee, four-time bestselling author, award-winning actress, filmmaker, singer, songwriter, entrepreneur, and philanthropist. She has performed in more than 20 films, numerous television shows, and several stage productions, appearing with stars such as Tom Hanks, Bryan Cranston, Debra Messing, Ben Stiller, George Takei, and Leonardo DiCaprio. Among the films she produced is *The Sand Castle,* in which she co-starred with multi-Emmy-Award winner Ed Asner. Cali is a former Miss North Hollywood Elite and the ambassador for the Save the Children of Tibet Project. She is the host and creator of the *Inspiration for Your Soul* podcast. Her vision is to be an outstanding artist and to inspire and heal in all she does.

www.calirossen.com

I Found My Purpose as a Marriage Expert

Linda Sam

At 58 years old, my fourth and final marriage led me to knowing my purpose in life—I am a marriage expert.

I have gotten married every which way a woman can get married. Each time I married, I did it differently. I stood in front of a justice of the peace at a courthouse. I had a Las Vegas wedding. I got married in a hotel with 22 bridesmaids. My fourth and final wedding was in my church with my beloved husband. This one will be my till-death-do-us-part marriage.

I know this is my last marriage because Tony is everything to me. He is exactly what I need. He is very comforting. He is amazing. He's funny. He keeps me laughing. He shares my love of music. These are things I have always looked for in a husband, I just hadn't found them until now.

I'm a firm believer that the Universe will return to you what you seek if you intentionally ask for it. My spirit was yearning to be with the right man. Then Tony literally showed up right in front of my face.

One night I was sitting at the bar listening to music. Tony was singing. We locked eyes. And that passion I saw in his eyes made me decide, *Wow, this is someone I'd like to get to know.* He felt the same way. In December 2019, we got married.

During a conversation with one of my friends, it dawned on me that this is my purpose. This is the reason I was born. It wasn't anything else I'd done in my life. It wasn't the jazz or the foundation I created to honor living jazz and blues legends. It wasn't being a parent advocate or a social media expert. It was being an expert on marriage.

My journey in this life that led me to four marriages gave me the vision to create a group where older couples can share experiences about being married.

And so, Married Tribe 55+ Couples Only was created. We help couples succeed in building lasting, lifelong, loving marriages. We're building a group of excited, encouraging, enlightening examples of educated couples enjoying life.

Tony and I host a weekly podcast of candid conversations about marriage. That is something that I can easily talk about. We have guest speakers on different topics such as sex, health, entertainment, night life, you name it. It's couples sharing our lives and our stories.

Your purpose is something that's God-given. It's the reason why God put you here. Everybody has a reason and a purpose for being here on life—you just have to find it.

When you get older, if you don't have a purpose, you don't feel excited about life or that you even have a reason to give back. If you have a purpose that you're energized by, that excitement makes you want to jump up out of the bed every day.

During our conversations with married couples, we also talk about leaving legacies and about finding your purpose.

You may be working a job, but it may not be your purpose. Are you always doing something that you like to do, but you never explored that as being your purpose? Maybe you just thought of it as something you like to do. No. That very well may be the theme that God has put you here to do, and you've not homed in on it yet.

To find your purpose, search for something that makes you

excited, something that won't go away. Something that continues to come up in your life. You may continue to shirk it off thinking that's not your purpose, but it keeps returning to you. If the same idea, that same excitement level, keeps coming to you, start exploring whether or not that's your purpose.

This realization of being a marriage expert didn't come to me initially. Years ago, if somebody had told me I would be married four times, I would have looked at them like they were crazy. But because that's been my life pattern, I now have this opportunity to have this purpose around marriage. It took a fourth and final marriage for my purpose to manifest.

I'm so excited that now, unequivocally, I'm an expert in marriage. With this budding community that we're building, I am looking forward to an even more exciting life enjoying this other side of 55.

You only get one life—live it. Make the best of it, whatever it is. You can't determine what your outcomes will be. When you live in the moment, the outcomes that are exactly what you need will manifest.

Be fearless. Take one day at a time. Stay positive. Stay grateful. Find your purpose. And keep living an exciting life.

❊ ❊ ❊

Linda Sam served her country as a Marine when she was in her 20s. Now, as she enters her 60s, she devotes her time to managing the Married Tribe 55+ Couples Only organization. During her podcast of the same name, she hosts candid conversations with couples about enjoying life and building lifelong, loving marriages. She has also hosted the online radio show *Jazzabrations*® *and Beyond!* Her passion for jazz led her to establish the Living Legend Foundation, which records, recognizes, and celebrates living jazz and blues legends. Linda is skilled in public relations, advertising, sales, and social media.

www.legacylifeleisure.com
www.facebook.com/MarriedTribe55PlusCouplesOnly.

Life's Too Short to Settle

Katrina Sawa

You can build the business of your dreams however you want it, but you do have to learn what to do and how to do it. It's not just going to drop into your head so that one day you'll miraculously know what to do to build a six- or seven-figure business.

First, understand that you deserve whatever it is you want. If you want to travel and speak all over the world, if you want to travel the country in an RV and work with clients on the phone, if you want to have an online business, if you want to stay home with your kids and have a business on the side—you can build it. You deserve it.

Maybe you are holding on to thoughts like these: *I have to go get a job. I have to keep the job that I hate. If I stay five more years, I'm going to get full retirement benefits.* Stop thinking you have to do business a certain way or that you have to have a J.O.B.

I've tried almost everything you could possibly imagine as I've built my business over the last 20 years. I've done it, failed at it, done it, succeeded at it, tweaked it, done it again, and didn't do it again. There's no magic pill. It takes a lot of work to grow your business.

Don't settle for things that don't make you happy. When you settle, you're going to be unhappy, and life's going to throw you some lemons.

Too many people are getting sick because they're miserable.

167

Illness can result from being unhappy and from being unhealthy—mentally or physically. Don't settle for being unhappy. Do the things you enjoy. Keep pushing after those dreams and trust that it will work out.

Invest in educating yourself about business. I invest in mentors and mastermind programs. I go to workshops and learn from people who are doing exciting things and making money at it. Then I apply the stuff I learn. That's the key.

When you're following someone who's actually being successful at the thing that they're teaching, implement their advice. There have been times when I've been stubborn and didn't take the advice I paid for. My own little ego was saying, *Thanks for the advice, but I'm going to do it MY way instead.* When I was too stubborn to take the experts' advice, that's when I would fail or not see the results.

Be consistent as you build your business. It's like with advertising. People want to run an ad for one day or one week, and think they'll attract business that way. That's not giving it enough time. You have to have frequency. You have to have an ad in people's faces on a regular basis.

It's the same thing with growing your business. Go to a networking event every month like clockwork. Talk to the same people so you can build and nurture those relationships. Be visible on the internet. Be in people's faces on social media and in their email inbox. Set up your system so you can be consistent and frequent. That's what turns them into clients.

I built the foundation for my highly successful coaching business almost 20 years ago on nothing but networking and follow up.

It's difficult to be in a funk or depressed when you have all kinds of clients calling you and counting on you. The busier you get with revenue-generating activities, and the more cash flow you bring in, the more clarity and confidence you'll have. So go get some clients, raise your rates, and go get some more.

As hard as you work at your business, remember to also work hard at your self-care. Rest and nutrition are the top two things for me, and then it's time with family.

When you love yourself and care for yourself, you will show up in a different light. You will attract better clients who want to pay you more. You will make more money, and you'll be doing something you enjoy. As the title of one of my books says, *Love Yourself Successful*.

Stop settling. Stop settling for relationships that are not supportive. Stop settling for a job that you hate. Stop settling for clients that suck the life out of you or who don't want to pay you what you're worth. Stop settling for not taking care of yourself. Stop settling for not having fun and joy in your life. That's not good enough, and it's not worth it. You deserve better.

Life is way too short to settle.

Katrina Sawa is the CEO and founder of Jumpstart Your Biz Now, and creator of the Jumpstart Your Marketing and Sales System. Ten of her 16 books have become international bestsellers, including *Love Yourself Successful, Jumpstart Your New Business Now,* and the *Jumpstart Your ____ (blank)* series. Through Jumpstart Publishing, Katrina helps entrepreneurs publish books that generate more clients and revenue. She founded the International Speaker Network, an educational networking group with thousands of members. She's been featured on the Oprah and Friends XM Radio Network, ABC, and The CW. Katrina was the National Collaborator of the year for the Public Speakers Association and was twice nominated for the Wise Woman Award by the National Association of Women Business Owners. She lives in Northern California with her husband and stepdaughter.

www.jumpstartyourbiznow.com

Believe in Yourself and Your Power

Joan L. Scibienski

I grew up in a very unstable, abusive home. I never knew from one day to the next, one hour to the next, one minute to the next, whether my father was going to explode and beat us or throw us down the stairs.

There was no outlet for this young Jewish girl in the very conservative Christian Indianapolis of the 1950s. If you went to the police about the abuse, you would have heard that the Bible says the man is in full control of his wife and children, and what happens in his home is up to him. I know, because that's what the police said to me.

I always had the feeling of helplessness. I asked my mother why she didn't leave her husband, my father. She looked at me like I was an alien, "And do what? I have no training in anything. I speak ragged English. How am I going to take care of you kids if I leave?"

All that impressed upon me that I would never allow myself to be that helpless, ever. So, of course, I walked out of my abusive father's home and married a man who was just as abusive. I continued that pattern.

I blamed myself for my husband's abuse. I kept thinking I was doing something wrong, that I was bad, that it would be okay if I could only be better.

The violence kept escalating until one day in 1972 he held a loaded gun to my head as he drove me toward the desert where he planned to blow my brains out. I jumped out of the moving car and took off running.

I talked to the police, but they would not let me file charges. "Oh, he's so sorry. He's having a bad day. He doesn't have work and he's depressed. He's been drinking and he just lost his temper. Go back and give this another try."

Here was another message like the one I heard when I complained about my father: *There must be a good reason for whatever the man does. If you're a good wife, you'll understand.* What?! I needed to let it go because he had a bad day?

The Universe had delivered a message: You have a choice. You can spend the rest of your life being helpless just like your mother, or you can do what it takes to make it work for you, no matter what happens.

If I had stayed in that abusive marriage, the whole rest of my life would not have turned out like it has. I would still be working in a menial job. I wouldn't have gotten my nursing degree or my psychology degree. I wouldn't have gone into private counseling practice. None of that would have happened, and I would not have the life I love.

I had a support system that believed in me, and they helped me believe in myself. Each time I didn't allow whatever happened to me hold me down, I learned another lesson about what I could do and how powerful I was.

My spirit guides helped me understand that these horrible events were not worthless. Every terrible experience enabled me to discover who I really am and who I wanted to become. It tempered me, it made me stronger, more loving, and more empathetic. I was not going to be helpless. I began to believe more in myself than I ever had before.

All this pushed me to my path. It didn't lead me to my path;

I kept being pushed. The Universe wanted me to know that I could use my experiences to help other people understand how incredibly powerful we all are if we accept personal responsibility and work toward what we really want.

The most important thing I could do to stop being an abused child and an abused wife was to forgive my abusers. I recognized the pain they'd had in their lives that caused them to take it out on me. When I did that, it set me free. It made me work harder to understand what propels a person to be who they are.

My father and his family went through a horrendous period when the Nazis took everything and killed several relatives before the family could escape from Germany. The trauma left its mark on him and led him to become exceedingly violent.

Knowing what I learned about PTSD, I better understand the actions of both my father and my ex-husband. It makes me incredibly sad, but there's no anger there.

People ask, "Don't you hate your ex-husband and your father?" No, I don't. How can I be angry with people who had so much pain? How can I hate them when they sacrificed so much to give me the lessons they gave me? Those lessons have enriched my life by helping me get on my path.

The process of forgiving and letting go is a whole lot easier when you can see the benefit of what you went through.

The first few decades of my life were absolutely horrendous. There were many, many days when all I could think about was wanting to die. Everything changed when I started believing in myself, when I understood the actions of my father and ex-husband and forgave them, and when I recognized the value of these life experiences to my growth.

I shifted from helplessness to feeling empowered by the Universe. All those difficult times brought me to the place and the person that I am today. And I'm happy about that.

Believe in yourself. Stop seeing yourself as a victim and start seeing yourself as victorious.

Forgive people in your past. Forgive people in your present. Forgive yourself. Let it go.

Learn from what you've experienced. Always look for what you can learn from a situation and utilize it to grow, gain more power, and move forward.

❋ ❋ ❋

Joan L. Scibienski's passion for over 40 years has been using her intuitive abilities working with clients throughout the world. She is the sole channel for the combined consciousness known as Equinox. In addition to her remarkable intuitive abilities, Joan uses her nursing and psychology degrees and experience as a certified substance abuse counselor to guide her clients so they can create their best lives. She has lectured and taught in the United States, Canada, and Europe, and hosts *The Circle Led by Joan Scibienski,* a spiritual membership group. Joan is the author of seven books, including *You Were Born Psychic: Unlocking Your Abilities to Create Your Best Life.*

The Circle Led by Joan Scibienski: www.thecirclegrp.com
www.intuitivedirections.net

My Forgiveness Journey

Laura Louise Smith

I was nine years old and asleep at home while my mother was out for the evening. A man broke into our house, molested me, and tried to kidnap me. Even though I fought him off and escaped, it scared me to my core when I realized I could have been a statistic if he had been the serial killer who was killing little girls who lived near me.

That traumatic event was the root of the fear and anger that haunted me for decades.

My hurt and anger came not so much because of what this stranger did to me, but because of the things that happened afterward. I had this notion that my parents should somehow know what I wanted and needed at the deepest levels. I wanted them to fix everything, and I got angry when they didn't. I didn't understand why they did what they did.

Feeling unloved and not understood, I created a tough external barrier of self-protection and isolated myself.

When I was 17, I ran away to marry a man my parents forbade me to marry. They disowned me, and we didn't talk for years. That was only the first time there were long stretches of silence between us.

By the time I was in my late 20s, my life was full of constant anger, constant manipulations, and constant road rage. I was a hothead and tried to start fights. I wanted power so I dated men I thought I could force to do things they didn't want to do. People who were humble or kind were weak people I could take advantage. It was ugly.

For years, more anger, more hurt, and more of life's disappointments kept getting cemented in me. I was out of control and I didn't have the power or the knowledge to deal with the root cause.

All of that gradually changed after my mother's passing. I started to realize through journaling and connecting with God that my parents had their own hurts that I knew nothing about. They hadn't gone through their healing journeys. They were living in their own hurt, and shame, and disappointment. They were human, not superheroes. They loved me the best way they could within their own messy lives.

They didn't change. I did.

It took me two solid years of arguing with God before I finally ended up on my father's doorstep to break the 15-year silence and ask for forgiveness. I knew my father wasn't going to apologize to me. I went there because I needed to drop all of my hurtful baggage and apologize for my piece of our separation.

I had been so isolated in darkness—so cut off, so harsh, so ugly. When forgiveness came into my life, I was lighter. I was airier. I started looking at things differently. I started viewing the world completely differently.

I found my purpose: to serve as a forgiveness advocate, share the power of forgiveness, and guide others on their own forgiveness journeys.

Here is a process that will help you get your forgiveness juices flowing as you start your own forgiveness journey.

- Decide who you need to forgive. Close your eyes and notice the first person that comes to mind. More times than not, it's a parent.

- Ask yourself if you are willing to forgive them. Are you willing to release the hurt and the anger and the disappointment? Are you ready to let it all go?
- If the answer is *yes*, start journaling. Write down whatever it is that hurt you, and your thoughts about it all. This process will help get those feelings out that you've suppressed for so long.

"I am angry because…"
"I am hurt because…"

- Examine what forgiveness looks like for you.

"I forgive you for..."
"I love you because..."

Forgiveness is not for those who hurt you. It's not about changing that other person. It's about how **you** are going to change. This is **your** journey to forgiveness and therefore creating your own peace.

I didn't know what peace was when I started my forgiveness journey. When I lived in hurt and unforgiveness, I was not in peace. *Peace* was a word that I saw on a cute plaque at someone's house. I didn't know what peace felt like. It took me decades to realize peace is an actual feeling, a state of being.

I still have a surface relationship with my dad. There's no depth, not like what I would really like. But the way I feel when talking to him, the way I conduct myself, and the mindset I have has completely changed. I now have peace.

He is who he is, and I am who I am. And it's okay that he didn't provide the things I wanted. He still has his baggage of hurt that he needs to work through. And I pray that he does that before he leaves this earth. But in the meantime, my peace is not going to be taken away because I didn't hear from my father what I so desperately wanted to hear.

Drop all of that unforgiveness you're holding on to. Forgive the people who have harmed you—not for them, but for you. The end result will not be to change that person. The end result will be your own peace.

It's going to take a little time to get to the light, but just keep walking. There were many times where I sat down on my road to forgiveness and said, "I don't want to play this right now. It's too much." There are other times where I stopped because it hurt, and I was a little winded. I needed to take a time out. Then I took another step forward. Now, every single day, I am in the light, no matter what is going on in my life.

You deserve to walk through forgiveness to the beauty and glory that's on the other side. I know because I've walked that narrow path.

❋ ❋ ❋

Laura Louise Smith is a forgiveness advocate, a mentor, author, and speaker. She made a promise to herself during her journey to healing that she would step up and serve as a powerful servant and authentic mentor to people who want to be free from the bondage of unforgiveness. To fulfill this mission, she founded Into the Light with Laura Louise. She holds a bachelor's degree in business administration and management, and a master's degree in organizational psychology.

www.intothelightwithlauralouise.com

The World is Waiting for You

Carol Soloway

During all my years as a chiropractor, I've helped hundreds of patients feel better and change their lives, some dramatically. Yet my biggest achievement is writing my international, bestselling children's book with my five-year-old granddaughter, Aria. The theme came from the great motivational speaker Les Brown's message of, "You've got to believe in yourself and your greatness." In *The Surprise Circus*, amazing things happen to a little girl when she believes in herself and is hungry to achieve her dream. She can do anything, even having something as amazing as her own circus.

I wish that I had learned this lesson way before I did. It would have taken so much of the struggle out of my life.

Having an absentee mother forced me to rely on myself from a young age. When I was 11, we moved to Florida where I didn't know anybody. I took the bus by myself whenever I wanted to go anywhere. I sold Girl Scout cookies door to door. When I was 17, I rode the bus into the city and got a job at Lord & Taylor. My parents didn't have a clue where I was or what I was doing. I didn't know that wasn't normal.

My mother passed more than 40 years ago, so I don't hear her voice anymore saying, "Who do you think you are? Do you think the world is waiting for you?" But I've internalized that message and have become my own critic. I don't need any help. I can do it myself. And I'm very good at it.

I've had this unshakable drive to prove myself. It's called Imposter Syndrome—thinking that I didn't deserve my success. I'd work hard to prove that I was good enough at something, and then another obstacle would cross my path. I'd work even harder to prove that I could do that. I felt like there was always something else to prove.

I earned my master's degree while I was teaching English. I went back to school to become a chiropractor while raising three children. After my divorce, when my children went to live with their father, I sold the house and used the money to start my practice. With only four months of overhead and my unshakable drive to prove myself, I built a successful practice.

The exterior world has thrown lots of difficulties at me. When outside stuff comes at me, I can deal with it. But it's the internal stuff that keeps challenging me. *Okay, what are you going to do next to prove that you're good enough to be here?*

I was a wife, but I must not have been a good wife because I got divorced.

I had three children, but I must not have been a good mother because I didn't have custody of them. I didn't tell anybody for 20 years because I was so ashamed.

I built a very successful chiropractic practice, but I always worried that no one would come in the next day.

When my first novel was launched in 2018, I made my wonderful, second husband promise we would move out of town if people thought the book was terrible.

When I wrote the book with my granddaughter, I was afraid parents wouldn't buy a children's book that was written by an author who had written women's novels.

For years, I held on to self-doubt, and continued to think I had to prove myself again and again. I thought I had to do everything myself. Nothing is a mark of success for someone who's so driven.

Not long ago, I learned a big lesson about asking for help. When COVID hit, I went from a 60-hour work week as a certified medical examiner to a zero-hour work week with no patients I could lay my hands on. I started feeling anxious when my frenetic life came to an abrupt halt. I suddenly became afraid of driving, and I panicked at night. That was not like me. I didn't know what to do.

I had never asked for help before. Never! My deep-seated childhood lesson was to only depend on myself. Even going through my divorce, I never had a therapist. I didn't feel deserving of spending money on such an extravagance. I would have felt extremely guilty if I'd allowed myself that luxury.

For the first time in my life, I consulted a psychologist. Her diagnosis: "I think you have cataracts. Go to your eye doctor." My ophthalmologist confirmed it. When the surgery solved the **real** problem, I stopped worrying about my mental health.

When we're as driven as I have been—and as so many women are—we don't give ourselves permission to ask for help. We've got to be willing to recognize when we need help and not feel guilty about asking.

I wish I had learned all this 20 years ago. We've got to create a shield for when the negativity comes in and when the self-doubt comes out.

In the last few years, I have invested in myself. I joined a mastermind and a critique group for writers. Now that I'm stepping in, it's astonishing to see how someone new is stepping out. I've asked people to help me promote my book, even though it's such a foreign concept, so far beyond my comfort level.

My children's book is the culmination of everything in my life. By teaching the message, *Believe in yourself*, I have found my voice, and I'm sharing the truth that I've been learning all my life.

Believe in yourself. Believe you can do it. Have unshakable drive. Do whatever it takes. Ask for help. Invest in yourself without guilt.

You **are** good enough. There's nothing you have to prove. The world **is** waiting for you.

❋ ❋ ❋

Dr. Carol Soloway is a chiropractor, qualified medical examiner, and a former English teacher. She published two bestselling novels before recently publishing the international bestselling children's book, *The Surprise Circus*, which she wrote with her five-year-old granddaughter. Dr. Carol has also authored an upcoming fantastical children's book series! She is president of the Orange County chapter of the International Association of Women and was IAW's 2018 Woman of Achievement. Carol is on the leadership team of the Orange County eWomenNetwork and was formerly a board member and one of the premier lecturers for the Academy of Forensic and Industrial Chiropractic Consultants. Her media experience includes being a paid, expert witness on *Judge Judy*, and interviews on Fox, ABC's *Morning Show*, and *The Morning Blend*. She is a permanent co-host on VoiceAmerica's *Transformation for Success* show. She has been featured in a host of magazines including *E The Magazine for Today's Female Executive, Dynamic Chiropractic,* and *Jewish Life*.

www.carolsoloway.com

Passionate About Making Babies

Diana Thomas

At 25, I was on track with my life's plan. I had a master's degree in architectural history, a job I loved, a great husband, a wonderful house, and even a white picket fence. Everything except children. I was doing things in the order I thought they should be done, but life wasn't happening the way I expected.

For the next 15 years, I felt like a science experiment. I struggled through countless medical interventions—surgeries, injections, and *in vitro* fertilization three times with my own eggs. I could not get pregnant. I ruled out adoption because I wanted to carry a child that had my husband's genes.

In the 1980s, infertility treatments were mostly uncharted territory. Every year, something new would come out, and the doctors would go, "Hey, let's try it on her because she's been around a while."

By the time I hit 40, I wondered if it was the end of the road. I couldn't overcome biology. This was the first wall I'd ever hit in my life. I had nothing but an empty nest, considerable debt, and a broken heart.

Finally, my doctor told me about a new technology called egg donation. Today that's more common, but the doctors knew little about it back then. With a shrug they said, "You can try this if you want." When I asked how to do that, they said, "We don't really know. We just know if you bring us an egg donor, we'll figure it out." I asked how to find an egg donor. And again, they replied, "We don't really know. You'll have to figure it out on your own."

It's my nature to ask a lot of questions so that I have enough information to make my own decision. But I wasn't getting any answers or appallingly inadequate answers from the doctors. They were covering up for how little they really knew about the process. As I continued to ask questions, I eventually found answers from a variety of other sources.

Very few people had heard of egg donation. Many people I talked to treated me like a freak because I wanted to carry a baby with another woman's genes. People came out of the woodwork with opinions that I wasn't asking for. I thought, *It's my life. It's my choice. I don't really care what you think.*

So, on my own, I figured out how to do it. In 1996, I gave birth to a healthy child who was one of the first 100 babies born with donor eggs in the United States. Two years later, I had twins through the same process.

After that success, infertility doctors asked me to find egg donors for their patients. Finding no established process, I realized this was an opportunity. I could help other women shorten their learning curve and show them that they had the power to make informed choices about their own family.

For a while, I was doing this for free while working as an architectural preservationist. When I realized I could stay home, run this new business, and raise the child that took me 15 years to have, I educated myself and started an egg donor agency.

I was so fortunate and felt very strongly that women should have the same opportunity I had to become a mother. I felt I needed to give back, and I did it by helping other women have choices and feel empowered to take this path.

When I started the first egg bank in the United States, I transitioned from a career that came from my education to a career that came from my passion. I am helping other women walk through the fear that our culture has attached to this whole process. Today, The World Egg and Sperm Bank, in our state-of-the-art donor facility, has brought joy and hope to thousands of families who could not have babies on their own.

Here are the most important lessons I've learned on my journey. . .

Find your passion in life. Be self-aware and open to possibility. Curiosity is the beginning of self-awareness—curiosity about yourself and curiosity about others without judgment. Observe yourself and listen to your thoughts. Ask yourself: *What does that mean? Why am I thinking that way?* Have conversations with other women. Listen to their stories. When you're self-aware and open to possibility, your passion will find you.

Believe in yourself. When nobody around you supports or believes in you, believe in yourself. Shut out those negative voices that are everywhere. It's a cultural reality that women business owners are treated differently than men. When I started my business, people treated me as if it were a hobby. Now younger women tell me I've inspired them. Accept that limitations are out there and do what you have to do to succeed. Don't be pulled off your path. Then find kindness and patience for yourself because it can be a tough road.

Don't let fear rule you. I had fears and questions from the beginning. *Am I doing this the right way? Maybe I won't be successful.* To get past my fear, I think of it not as an enemy but as a nuisance. I don't let it paralyze me or obscure my goals. When I feel fear, I close my eyes and feel what's really deep inside of me. I ask myself: *What is there to really be afraid of? Is it real? What's the worst thing that could happen?* I recognize that I can manage the emotions. I give myself five minutes to feel doubt and fear and to wallow in self-pity or regret. Then I say: *Okay, that's done. Now I'm going to move on.* It works. I look at fear as a gift.

When you move around fear, there's always a silver lining. Trust your gut. Trust who you are.

Diana Thomas graduated magna cum laude from Arizona State University with a master's degree in architectural history. For over 15 years, she enjoyed a career as an architectural historian for the province of Alberta, Canada. She loved her work, but her desire to have a family changed the direction of her future. Using her experience from the 20-year-long journey to have a child, she created a business that caters to the personal needs of intended parents and brings the best quality of care to donors. Under Diana's direction, The World Egg and Sperm Bank focuses solely on egg and sperm donors. It is the only egg and sperm bank in the US that manages all donor screening, clinical processes, and shipments from its state-of-the-art facility. Her compassion coupled with her personal experience has helped thousands of couples worldwide conceive their families with the assistance of egg and sperm donors.

www.theworldeggandspermbank.com

Exercise Your
Self-Love Muscle

Mellissa Tong

Under a brilliant blue sky, I settled in for a solitary drive in my bright red sports car. The top was down, and mine was the only car on this narrow, winding country road. As I rounded a curve, I sailed past a little girl standing by the side of the road. I knew I must go back to her. I backed up, backed up, backed up—a very long way. I picked her up and hugged her tightly, telling her, "I will never leave you behind." As I tucked my little girl into the safety of the black leather seat next to me, I knew I must protect her and heal her childhood wounds—my childhood wounds. And we drove off together to continue our journey.

Chinese parents don't show love through physical touch or through words—at least mine didn't. I received no confirmation that I was loved. I always felt that I wasn't really wanted. I came a month early, and my parents were so unprepared. My sister came along eight and a half years later, after my mother made a promise to my dying grandmother that I wouldn't be the only child.

My sister was a promise—the one who was wanted. I was the unwanted one. It was very easy to think that way as a kid. My mom treated my sister completely differently than she treated me. My mom would put me up on the chair so I could be tall enough to wash dishes. I had to clean the windows and doors. She never made my sister do that.

She still treats us differently.

During my childhood, I developed some sort of mechanism to not feel emotions, and I carried that into my adult life.

After college, I moved from my home in Hong Kong to Los Angeles. I completed a master's degree. I got married. I had two successful careers—as a news anchor and then my own production company.

But when I realized that I wasn't feeling fulfilled, I started looking for the missing ingredient that would take my business to the next level. None of the programs I attended taught me the one business trick I thought would grow my business the way I wanted it to.

I heard somebody say that if something doesn't work on your business that means something's not working on the personal level. I didn't know what that meant, but I kept searching.

The missing piece showed up at a networking event a few years later when I won an impromptu drawing for a three-day women's workshop. I knew nothing about this event. I didn't even google it to find out more. I just cancelled everything on my schedule and went.

It was not what I expected.

On the first day, they talked about how each of us has our "little girl," our inner child that we carry with us. The powerful vision I had that day of my little girl standing by the side of the road sent me home crying.

I locked myself in the bathroom and cried and cried and cried. I couldn't stop. I had never cried that hard my whole life.

At the end of the program, I signed up for a year-long program. I had never done anything like that before. I'd never even gone to a therapy session and had no idea what personal development was about. The only thing I knew was that the workshop was having a profound effect on me.

Call it destiny. Call it God. Call it whatever. Something was telling me I needed to do this. I didn't know if it was going to help me, but I could not let this pass.

Over the years I had lost touch with myself. When I imagined picking up my little girl, I was finally able to connect with her—and with my childhood hurts and my emotions.

Because I never felt emotions from my parents, I did not learn to exercise that self-love muscle. I had nobody around me who was using those muscles or functioning at an emotional level who could show me how important that was. I pushed my emotions aside for so long. Finally, when the gate was cracked open, everything started moving quickly.

It wasn't about learning a magical business trick. Going through my personal growth and letting go of a lot of what I had been hanging on to for so long is what changed my whole business. My life is now so different. The way I talk to people is different. The way I listen is different. The way I connect with people is different. The way I interview people is different. The way I approach a story is different. Everything is different.

Self-love is to truly embrace yourself and accept both your strengths and weaknesses. It's about not beating yourself up. Self-love is a muscle everyone has, but you must exercise it so you can call on it anytime you want. Because I've done so much work with it, when something doesn't go my way, I can pick myself up pretty quickly and easily.

Here's how I practice self-love. I look into my own eyes in a mirror and say things that I like about myself. "You're good at this. You're good at that." I end by saying, "I love you. I love you, Mellissa Tong, I love you." When I first started doing it, I had tears in my eyes. I never had learned how to love myself. It wasn't easy. But I kept at it, and I got there.

After my morning meditation and prayer, I kiss myself and say out loud, "I love you." This sets the tone and opens me up to embrace each new day that's bursting with endless possibilities. It fills me with limitless love for myself, for the people I meet, and for the gift that I want to take into the world.

Remember that the world is communicating with you, as it did when the women's workshop dropped into my life. It's up to you to truly listen and become aware of those small cues that are trying to get your attention. Take five or 10 minutes every day to listen to your body and see how you're feeling. Have that check-in to ask yourself: *How am I feeling right now? Am I happy? Am I frustrated? Am I feeling off?*

Be open to being guided. Don't reject it. Don't block it. It will eventually lead you to where you're supposed to be.

Your own cup has to be full so that you can contribute to the world. Fill your cup by exercising your self-love muscle and truly loving yourself.

❈ ❈ ❈

Mellissa Tong is an award-winning film and video director/producer, business storyteller, three-time Amazon bestselling author, and international speaker. In 2000, she founded DuckPunk Productions, Inc., a creative marketing and content production company, boosting sales up to 400% for her clients and winning awards such as Clio, ADDY, Telly, and a dozen more from film festivals across the country. She has over 25 years of experience both in front of and behind the camera. Her work includes branding and marketing, customer communications, television commercials, and branded content for some Fortune 500 companies including Nissan, Verizon, and Wells Fargo. She earned her bachelor's degree in her hometown of Hong Kong and a Master of Fine Arts at California Institute of the Arts after moving to the United States in 1991. Mellissa began her career as a news anchor/reporter/producer at the International Channel in Los Angeles. While on the job, she interviewed thousands of people from all walks of life and covered over 1,200 stories.

www.duckpunk.net
www.rockstaroncamera.com

Repurposing Pain to Peace

Victoria Valentino

By the age of 25, I'd experienced enough tragedy to fill several lifetimes. I come from a long line of strong women, yet my early life of privilege did little to prepare me for what was to come.

I spent the first years of my adult life being objectified—told to just stand there and look pretty, but not to say anything intelligent and spoil it.

The man I married when I was so very young took nude pictures of me and submitted them to a magazine I'd never heard of. By the time *Playboy* magazine chose me as a centerfold, he had already started hitting me. My plans to flee fell apart when I discovered I was pregnant.

By the time my son was a year old, I was a Playboy celebrity. Leveraging my recognition, my husband trafficked me to Hollywood celebrities and politicians.

I'm still dealing with physical injuries from the violent beating he inflicted on me the day I finally escaped with my son.

Each day at the Playboy Club when I put on my bunny costume, I put on a happy face so I could earn a living for my son and me. I didn't understand I was suffering from PTSD. I just had to put one foot in front of the other and keep going.

People were not kind to a single white mother with a mixed-race child. When my beautiful son, Tony, drowned two weeks after his sixth birthday, I begged God to take me. A few weeks later, Bill Cosby took advantage of my vulnerability, and drugged, kidnapped, and raped me.

Life looked at me and saw that I was not following the purpose I was put here to follow. It ripped the rug out from under me and said, "Let's see what you're going to do with your life now that you have nothing left." It created motion. It created energy. It created change. And opportunity.

My survival instinct somehow got me through all that, and more.

My soul needed these lessons to turn me toward my purpose in this lifetime—to be a teacher, and to serve others by sharing the lessons I learned. And through that process, to heal myself.

My healing came in layers. It wasn't just one deadline that I met, and from then on out everything was cool. There have been many different layers in which I discovered parts of myself coming alive: feeling the love of my second husband's family; focusing on clear, short-term goals and getting positive reinforcement in my college courses; and getting involved with new people in a fresh environment. Each layer put me in a frame of mind and a state of grace that allowed me to accept the next layer of healing.

Graduating with honors at 42 started me on my path as a registered nurse. I felt healthy. I possessed a new zest for life that I didn't have in my 20s when I was busy just trying to survive. As I aged, I learned to find joy through service to others.

Combining my own experience of pain and grief and suffering with my training as a home hospice nurse and bereavement facilitator, I've been able to help people who were losing everything—losing their lives—become comfortable in the profound beauty of not knowing, of being at ease with death. For over 30 years, my role has been that of a midwife at the other end of life.

Working with others through the profound grieving process

has helped me heal from my son's death.

In the late 90s, I was speaking to groups and magazines about sexual assault, though I didn't identify Cosby. As a registered nurse and a Playboy icon, I had reached a place of professional respect in stereo. People wanted to know what I had to say and asked me for advice. Women and men from all over the world reached out to me, sharing their stories for the very first time of being victims of incest, rape, and domestic abuse. They trusted me. What more could I ask for than to be trusted by a stranger? I was able to help others by giving them a little something of myself. If I died today, I know I have done something of value.

Another layer of healing unfolded in 2014 when the world started believing what women had claimed for years—that Bill Cosby was a rapist. I began speaking more publicly about him assaulting me. By then, I felt strong within myself, and knew the time was right to tell that part of my story.

That helped me heal my own pain and shame while helping others do the same. I have learned that the creative process slows me down and gives me time to heal. Doing creative things with my hands, things that keep me physically occupied, has also helped me heal—things like crafts, pottery, crochet, and decoupage. The result is something tangible that I have created, something beautiful and useful. I realize now that I've used creativity as a tool to heal. After my six-year-old son drowned, I continued to hand sew a quilt that I had been making for him.

When I publicly shared that I had been raped by Cosby, I started crocheting again, something I hadn't done since I was a teenager. I made some of the most bizarre looking plant hangers you've ever seen. Through both of his trials, I sat in the court room and crocheted to keep myself calm.

Connecting with nature facilitates healing. Nature has seasons just like life has seasons. When you're traumatized and under stress, you're in the winter of your life. When you understand nature, you know that no matter how long winter lasts, spring always comes.

During that wintertime, when you can't see your way through, go out in nature. Take a walk. Go to the park. See what other people are growing in their gardens. Steal a few little pieces of geranium or a piece of a succulent and stick it in your own garden. Dig in the dirt. Plant a flower seed, and watch it bloom. Grow an avocado seed. Put an old, sprouted potato in a little flowerpot on your windowsill. Grow the seeds from your Halloween pumpkin. Watch a plant give birth to a succulent tomato that you can eat and enjoy.

There's something so therapeutic about seeing things grow. Gardening is how I get rid of pent-up rage. It does wonders for your soul and connects you back with who you are.

Become your own mother. Nurture yourself. Don't wait for somebody else to make it all better for you. Do something nice for yourself, something nourishing and nurturing. Turn off the phones. Stay in bed with a good book and a hot cup of tea. Don't wait for someone else to give you flowers. Buy yourself some roses. Wrap yourself up in love. Stand in front of the mirror and say, "Damn, you look good today, girl," or, "That was a smart thing you did." Be good to yourself. Love yourself.

We're put here to learn the soul's lessons. Everything that comes to us, as painful and horrible as it might be on the surface, always carries a lesson. We need to look for the lessons to make ourselves better humans, to be more empathetic and compassionate, to see that core thread that connects every living human being on the planet, and to become more harmonious with the Divine, to repurpose pain to peace.

❋ ❋ ❋

Victoria Valentino is a keynote speaker and media personality. She shares her journey as a multi-rape survivor, sex trafficking survivor, and vintage *Playboy* centerfold, all before she was 22. She moved on to become an actress, talk show host, writer, singer, dairy goat farmer, and registered nurse. She home-birthed her youngest daughter while living on the farm. Victoria is most widely known as a major media voice and outspoken survivor of sexual assault by Bill Cosby. She is raising the consciousness about rape culture and transformational healing through her work as an ambassador for several organizations including Promoting Awareness Victim Empowerment (PAVE), Hope Pyx Global for sex trafficking, and the Never Walk Alone Foundation. She helped promote a law to abolish the statute of limitations on rape and sexual assault in California, which became effective January 1, 2017. Recently, she lent her voice to a campaign by Joyce Short's Consent Awareness Network (CAN) to pass into law a New York Senate Bill establishing a legal definition of consent as Freely Given, Knowledgeable and Informed Agreement. Writing her memoir and describing how she has repurposed the difficult parts of her life has proven to be a painful and therapeutic process. It's certain to be an inspiring book when it's finished.

Email: vvalentino1@earthlink.net

Remember to Use Your Lived Experiences (Dr. Pat's R.U.L.E.)

Patricia Van Pelt

I ran for mayor in Chicago in 2010 because the silence around what was happening in our communities was so loud.

We couldn't let our children play outside. We couldn't walk to the grocery store if there was even one person anywhere near our home. We were struggling with unemployment, especially young Black men. I knew if I didn't say something about what was really happening in our communities, people would think they really didn't matter. I felt a responsibility to help people do something about what was going on.

My mother was the one who inspired me. My dad couldn't work anymore after he was in a terrible car accident. In order to pay the rent and buy food for seven children, my mom worked in the daytime and went to school at night. We moved into Cabrini-Green, a notorious housing project—one of the worst in the whole city for crime, drugs, and violence. In five years, she got a college degree, got a good job, bought a home, and moved us out of the project.

Watching her made me understand, as I've gone through challenges in my own life, that I am not defenseless, and that there is an answer when I reach out beyond what I think are the parameters in my life.

When I was 10 years old, I was watching television shows like *Father Knows Best* and *By the Light of the Silvery Moon*. Everybody on TV was Caucasian. Everything was clean and pretty, and everybody was happy. But where I lived, everything was dirty and trashy. There were frequent shootings and killings. Everybody was Black. What they were projecting on television was not reality for the people I knew.

I started searching, knowing there had to be more to life. Not having any real guidance at home, I unplugged from school, and dropped out at 15.

I started using drugs when I was 11, but didn't realize I was an addict until I was 19 when I couldn't get the drugs. I never intended for my life to be like that. I always said, "I'm going to grow up, and make a lot of money, and help the poor." That was my mindset.

But here I was at a point where I couldn't even help myself. I was a high school dropout, unemployed, unwed mother, drug addict, and homeless. I looked at myself in the mirror and thought, *Where are you going? You're going to die if you don't get off this road.*

Once I realized I was addicted, I struggled to find what was real. I was supposed to help people, yet I was in no condition to even help myself.

During this difficult time, I worked in the steel mills. Every time a machine broke, they sent the broken part to the manufacturer. When the new part came back, the machine would always work again. There was never a machine that couldn't be fixed.

So, I started thinking, *I'm broken. I must be missing some parts. Who is **my** manufacturer? God made me, so maybe he can help.* I didn't grow up having a relationship with God or Jesus, but I went to church to see if I could find a part to fix me.

That first day at the Pentecostal church when the preacher prayed for me, my life went before me in seconds. I had a powerful encounter with God. All of a sudden, I knew that the drug abuse, the lying, the stealing, the cheating, the way I was living, all the things I did were wrong.

When I woke up the next morning, instead of wondering, as I usually did, how I was going to get high, I heard my mind say, *You don't need drugs anymore.* That desire was suddenly gone. At 21 years old, I started a brand-new life that I've lived for more than 40 years.

During the campaign for mayor in 2010, I asked one of the other candidates where she had been for the last 20 years, and why we hadn't seen her try to solve the problems in our neighborhood. She said, "The reason you don't know where I've been is because you've been on crack for 20 years." It didn't matter to her that by that time I had a PhD and was a certified public accountant. Or that I had been clean for over 30 years.

But her trying to pull me down is exactly what boosted me up. Before the mayor's race, nobody knew who I was. Because of what she said, my name recognition went higher than any other candidate in that race. I lost the mayor's race but had the visibility to run for state senator.

Had she not brought up my past, I would not have beat a well-financed incumbent for that senate seat in 2012. My past wouldn't have happened had my mom not left us by ourselves while she was trying to get us out of the project and build a better life for us.

I see everything as part of the solution in our lives.

I have a belief I call Dr. Pat's R.U.L.E.: **Remember to Use your Lived Experiences.** My past is the thing I can go back to and get reinforcement when I feel like I can't make it. I go back to past experiences and say, *I remember when I was there and thought there was no way out. And yet I came out. I can come out now because I did it before.* Something always comes forth to bring the deliverance we need from the challenges we have.

Your past experiences are your power source. Most people don't want to think about what they've been through and the horrible things they suffered. They don't realize those things reveal the power that you had. Now you're stronger than ever before, and you need to remember to use those lived experiences.

As a state senator, I continue to work to empower people. Because I've had all those experiences, I'm able to relate to people in a way that they see as authentic. I can talk about things other legislators don't know anything about. They haven't been there. I'm bringing the voice of ordinary people to the table of government.

I'm not ashamed of where I came from. I'm not afraid of the past. I'm not even afraid of the future. I had times when I was afraid of the future, but I don't have that anymore. I look back at my past and realize, *Girl, there's nothing you can't do.* My mother is even more proof.

Never be afraid to look at yourself for who you are. What you went through is not useless. It's not a disgrace. It's your power source.

Never lose faith in yourself. Everything that you need is in you already. The power you need to realize your dreams and to walk in your purpose is there in your lived experiences. You just have to dig it out.

❈ ❈ ❈

Dr. Patricia Van Pelt has served as a senator in the Illinois General Assembly since 2013. She is an entrepreneur, author, transformation coach, real estate developer, certified public accountant, community activist, evangelist, and a lifelong resident of Chicago. Her diverse background includes working as steelworker and union steward, co-founding Ambassadors of Christ Church, and founding TARGET Area Development Corporation, a grassroots social justice organization. Dr. Pat had dropped out of school by age fifteen, but went on to earn her GED, an associate degree in natural science, a bachelor's degree in public administration, a master's degree in human services administration, and a doctorate in management of non-profit agencies.

www.senatorvanpelt.com
www.drpat.net

Act Like You Know What You're Doing

Deirdre Virvo

I tend to jump into things before I know everything because I know I can figure it out as I go along.

When I started my short-sale business, it was my first foray into full-time real estate investing. I took a course, quickly formulated my business plan, and got everything set up as fast as possible because I needed money as fast as possible. Once it was set up, I had to tell people that I negotiate short sales even when I'd never negotiated a single one before.

How to start? I couldn't sit in my ivory tower and expect people would come to me. I had to go to them and tell them. So, I said to myself, *Okay. Tell everybody you meet today that you do short sales. Give them your card.*

At nine o'clock that morning, I was in line at the post office. I was nervous because, honestly, I didn't know how to do short sales. But I was going to be telling people I did. As I was finishing my transaction, I said to the post office lady behind the counter, "Oh, by the way, I negotiate short sales. If you know anybody that needs help or is underwater with their house, here's my card."

She said, "Can you wait a minute? I want to talk to you. Can you meet me at the side door?" I waited until she finished her line of customers, and she came over to the side door. She said, "I need a short sale." No way! The first person I talked to was going to be my first customer? I wasn't thinking it would be her—but it was.

The market had just crashed, and people needed help. Knowing that I was helping people, my fear was eliminated. I started telling everybody I talked to that I handled short sales, and if they knew anybody that needed help, send them to me. I became a short sale queen in my area and started teaching courses to real estate agents.

Now that I've helped over a thousand people get out of foreclosure, I think of myself as a social worker. I focus on helping people and do whatever it takes to get them through. If they need to get rid of furniture, if they need to find the next place to live, if they need help with their probate work, I have done everything to help them. I love it.

This is a business where you don't live and learn, you live, and live, and live, and never learn it all. I keep looking for the "now-you've-got-this" thing. But there's always a new issue with every short sale.

I'm okay with saying I don't know things. I'm okay with saying I have to figure it out. I'm okay with making mistakes. Mistakes happen and I fix them. That's all. Whatever happens is fixable.

I'm not pretending I'm something I'm not, but I act like I know what I'm doing, and I figure it out. Everything is doable.

Be the first to help people whenever they need something. If it has nothing to do with you or your business, help them anyway. You never know when an opportunity is going to present itself or where it will lead.

Even talking to people about nothing that has to do with work, just helping them with their other issues, has gotten me private money lenders because they know me, like me, and trust me. I may not even talk to them at first about what I do or what they have. When they find out what I do, they'll say, "What? Do you flip houses? Do you need an investor?" So, it's a win/win situation. Helping others helps you as well. It comes back to you tenfold.

When things don't seem to be working out, remember it's temporary. Don't let naysayers get in your head.

When I was going through a divorce and was a million and a half dollars in the hole, people told me I should be working 24 hours a day. I shouldn't get a nice apartment. I shouldn't be having fun. They'd say, "How are you happy when you're not even at ground zero yet? You're still in a big hole."

I told them, "I know I'm going through a lot. I lost my house, and lost my husband, and lost all my money. But I'm still going to have fun and enjoy my life even while I'm in debt. It could take a while to build back up, but I'm not going to sit around moping for the next few years. It's temporary."

It took me seven years, but I paid off that debt. I got another house and bought other properties. Meanwhile, I was happy with everything else going on in my life.

I found a lot of free things to do. I ushered at the local playhouse that brings in national plays. I love Broadway shows and used to go to every show. But with no money, I still wanted to have fun. So, I volunteered to usher, and got to see the plays for free.

Things happen, but you can still be happy along the way. You can lose your money. You can lose your health. You can lose your husband. You can lose whatever. But you still can be happy because you have a million other things to be grateful for.

The setbacks are temporary if you make them temporary. If you just sulk and mope and ruin your life, that's one way of dealing with it. But if you make it a temporary glitch, then you can move on.

Money comes and goes. You make it. You spend it. You lose it. You make it. It doesn't matter. You can get more anytime. That's just money. A bigger issue is losing people or your health. If you have to lose something, losing your money is the best thing to lose. I'd rather lose my money than my eyesight, or my friends, or my house, or my family. I can always make more money.

Anytime you go into new territory, it can be scary. Believe in yourself. Jump in. Have a can-do attitude. Say *yes* as much as possible. Act like you know what you're doing. Figure it out as you go along. And just start somewhere.

❋ ❋ ❋

Deirdre Virvo has been a full-time real estate investor and entrepreneur since 2007, after leaving her successful career as an advertising executive and agency owner. Her company, CT Property Network, specializes in negotiating short sales, renovating and flipping houses, buying rentals, and acquiring and holding residential and commercial buildings. She prides herself in the fact that she has helped more than a thousand families avoid foreclosure. Deirdre wrote and teaches a continuing education course on buying distressed properties, short sales, auctions, and foreclosures for real estate agents in Connecticut. She is a founding member of the SoCT Real Estate Investors Association. She is the coauthor of two books: *Be a Success Maverick*, and *Home to Home, The Step by Step Senior Housing Guide*. Her passion for seniors led her to open Just Like Home, LLC, a boutique senior residence for seniors with memory care needs. Deirdre teaches workshops to help seniors and their families create a housing roadmap to honor seniors' wishes and prepare for eldercare.

www.ctpropertynetwork.com
www.justlikehomellc.com

Don't Live Your Life On "Someday I'll. . ."

Mary Jo West

If I had had balance earlier on in my life, things would have been different. I don't want to live in regret for my mistakes, but the one thing I would change would be to not make my job the only thing in my life.

After spending a year off from college and traveling the country as Miss Atlanta, I decided to get a degree in journalism. It was the early 70s, and the timing was perfect. The FCC had just changed the rules and insisted that television stations hire minorities and women.

In 1976, I was hired by the CBS affiliate in Phoenix as the first primetime television anchorwoman in the city. Phoenix was one of the last conservative bastions to hold out and not allow women to do a primetime newscast. Women were allowed to be reporters, or do weather, or maybe a cut-in at noon. But no one dared to sit at that anchor desk next to Bill Close, the news legend in Phoenix for many years. His ratings were fantastic all by himself. He didn't need someone to sit next to him, especially a young blondie.

It was hard—for both of us. As I've aged, I've been better able to step into his shoes. Maybe he felt threatened by the changes that were going on. But at the time, I had a very difficult time working alongside a co-anchor and a boss who didn't want me there.

I was only 27, but I had worked so hard to get to where I was. I worked harder than anyone else, male or female, to prove to Bill and our viewers that I was more than just an arm decoration. Sadly, many of my detractors at first were women. A lady from the retirement community of Sun City called the station and said that I was a blonde-headed tomato and should go home and cook supper for my husband.

It was very important to me that people saw me as more than a "blonde-headed tomato." I wanted to talk about issues that were vital and to report stories of substance. I didn't just stand in front of a camera and read the news. I went out and investigated significant issues that were not being covered.

I felt like I was being watched very closely. So, in order to do all the things I felt I needed to do, I worked many, many, many 18-hour days. I was almost fearful to go on vacation thinking they'd replace me while I was gone. I kept pushing and pushing and pushing.

That F-word dominated my life. No, not THAT F-word, but F-E-A-R. *Was I good enough? Was I pretty enough? Was I slim enough? Was I smart enough?* We were in a profession where we were judged so much more than other professions.

Finally, I just had to let that go of the fear and bring ME to the table—nobody else.

From the age of nine on, I did things that other people were afraid to do. I always pushed that envelope. In seventh grade I started a school newspaper, became president of the student council, and on and on and on. I'm the black sheep of the family because I left the nest in Atlanta and came out to Phoenix. I've always been an overachiever—and ambitious.

At one time I think I would have run over my grandmother to win an Emmy award. Now I don't even know where mine are— probably in a box somewhere.

I was so determined to succeed in my career that I faltered along the way. I became my job while my marriage and my personal life suffered.

My precious first husband, Jim, said I collected wounded birds. I met so many people while doing my stories. And on weekends, I would go out and help them instead of spending quality time with Jim or taking care of myself.

One night, when I dragged myself home to our little apartment at 3 a.m., Jim was sitting up in bed. He looked at me and said, "Jo, everyone wants a piece of my lady, and all I ever get are the leftovers." I just balled.

I wasn't able to achieve a balance in either of my marriages. What got in the way was simply the fact that I had a lover, and that lover was my job.

I wish I had learned the art of saying *no* sooner. "No" is a complete sentence. That's all you have to say. I never, ever said *no* to any of my bosses.

That led to me covering the presidential conventions in 1980, a first for local news in Phoenix. That meant not sleeping for five days when I was covering the Republican convention in Detroit. The producers wanted more and more TV spots. They wanted radio news stories. I was afraid to say, "Hey, maybe instead of reporting six items a day, why don't we try four?" I did whatever they asked, even to the point of hurting myself.

You've got to learn to say *no*. You don't need to even give an excuse. You can do it in a polite way. Set limits on what you're willing to do. Here's what works: "No, but this is what I **can** do for you." We women are such people pleasers that we are afraid to say *no*.

Later, when I was doing a lot of speaking along with reporting, anchoring, and community work, I practiced a different approach. When someone asked me to do something, I would give them three or four names of other people to ask, people I thought would welcome that opportunity. Later on in my life, I started doing a really good job at saying *no*.

I've been mentoring young people for over 40 years. And when I meet someone who wants to get into this business, the first thing I ask them is, "What do you know about having balance in your life?"

Whatever career you're in, always remember that balance comes first. Balance means putting people first, not your job.

Don't live your life on "Someday I'll. . . " *I'll be happy someday if I get the right job. I'll be happy someday if I meet the right person. I'll be happy someday if I lose 20 pounds.*

Be kind to yourself. And most of all, find joy in living in the present moment.

Mary Jo West has been called the First Lady of TV News in Phoenix. In 1976, she became the city's first prime-time female anchor. She also anchored CBS News' Night Watch in New York City. She has opened many doors for the women who followed her. In addition to two Rocky Mountain Emmy Awards, Mary Jo won her industry's top awards: the Peabody, 13 Arizona Press Club awards, and the national Gracie Allen Award from American Women in Radio and TV. She was the first newswoman inducted into the Arizona Broadcasters Hall of Fame. The City of Phoenix honored her with the Martin Luther King Living the Dream Award for her work fighting discrimination against the mentally ill. Before retiring, she ran her own communications company and worked for St. Vincent de Paul, the State of Arizona, the Roman Catholic Diocese of Phoenix, and the City of Phoenix. After five years in retirement, and in need of some stimulation, she started working at the information booth at Sky Harbor airport where she gets to do what she loves—help people. Say hello to her when you're flying through Phoenix, or contact her at:

Email - westmolly48@gmail.com

Stay Connected with Women Who Push the Limits

Women Who Push the Limits is more than a book or two, it's a powerful project. Based initially on in-depth interviews with 50 women who push the limits, their stories are being made into wonderful podcasts and YouTube videos. Watching and listening to these interviews, you'll get to know even more about these women and their wisdom. Their stories—the challenges and the advice—are bursting with lessons that are being incorporated into presentations, workshops, and coaching sessions that will help women apply these lessons in their own lives and allow us to stay connected with others who push the limits. **Together we can build a community of Women Who Push the Limits.**

Learning about other women's challenges and victories helps us all realize how resilient we are and helps us build confidence that we each have the courage and the strength to deal with whatever challenges cross our path.

You are invited to become part of our community of like-minded women.

Browse our website:
www.womenwhopushthelimits.com

Sign up for our email list so you're among the first to know about events, programs, and future books.

***Subscribe to our Facebook group, YouTube channel*, and** *Podcast*: Women Who Push the Limits

Acknowledgments

This book would not have happened without the support of these wonderful people:

First, the most important person in my life, my husband Mike, who has my deepest love, gratitude, and appreciation. He has always believed in me, encouraged me, and backed me up for more than 45 years. He feeds me a great dinner every night so that I don't sit at my computer until midnight munching only pistachios or popcorn.

To Connie Deutsch for believing in me, for sparking the idea for this book, and for making me believe I could do it.

To my awesome editor, publisher, and friend Thea Rademacher of Flint Hills Publishing who guided me through every step of this process, assured me that I **am** a writer, and laughed with me when I struggled with that perfection gene. She has challenged me to be a better writer and showed me how to move in that direction. She demonstrated infinite patience, wise counsel, and honest feedback, going far beyond what any other publisher would do. Thank you for being a true partner and sharing this journey with me.

When this project was in its embryonic stage, Craig Duswalt gave me the opportunity to stand up in front of the room and share the idea with ninety people in his Rock Your Life MasterMind, a group I had recently joined. That was the first time I'd talked about this idea with people I barely knew. I'd hardly even talked about it to my friends! I was overwhelmed by the enthusiasm and positive support that poured from this group. As I walked up to my hotel room afterward, I said to myself, *Well, I guess I really am doing this.* It started to feel real. Thanks, Craig, for surprising me with a hot seat that day, and for connecting me with some amazing women. It was meant to be.

To everyone who offered suggestions and contact information for someone awesome to interview, thank you for helping me expand my reach.

Many, many thanks to my dear friends and relatives who encouraged me to write this book and who haven't crossed me off their list because I've ignored them for so long. You know who you are, and you know I love you.

About the Author

Lynn W. Murphy, M.Ed., is a speaker, author, and leadership development expert who works with organizations and success-minded individuals to accelerate their performance and more quickly achieve their goals by mastering interpersonal skills and team dynamics. She is the president and founder of Key Innovative Business Solutions.

You may have seen Lynn sharing customer service tips on the Fox 10 Phoenix morning show or read her #1 Amazon bestselling book *7 Keys to Improving Your Customer Service*. She has worked with organizations such as Marriott International, US Bureau of Land Management, and Ford Motor Company.

Inspired by the many remarkable women who are claiming leadership roles in business and politics, she created the Women Who Push the Limits movement to inspire, motivate, and empower women to claim their power. Lynn has gathered stories from extraordinary women who have created success in spite of, or because of, the challenges they've had in their lives. Through these stories you'll learn to **find your voice, speak your truth, and change the world.**